VAIL PUBLIC LIBRARY

1 16 0001236 03

W9-DFU-046

J 951.9 BAC
Bachrach, Deborah, 1943-
The Korean War

145928

1650

1/98-2   96

Vail Public Library
292 West Meadow Drive
Vail, CO 81657

The Korean War

Books in the America's Wars Series:

The Revolutionary War
The Indian Wars
The War of 1812
The Mexican-American War
The Civil War
The Spanish-American War

World War I
World War II: The War in the Pacific
World War II: The War in Europe
The Korean War
The Vietnam War
The Persian Gulf War

The Korean War

by Deborah Bachrach

America's WARS

Lucent Books, P.O. Box 289011, San Diego, CA 92198-0011

VAIL PUBLIC LIBRARY

For my sons: Jamison, David, and Daniel

Library of Congress Cataloging-in-Publication Data

Bachrach, Deborah, 1943-
 The Korean War / by Deborah Bachrach.
  p.   cm. — (America's wars)
 Includes bibliographical references and index.
 Summary: Explains how America was involved in the Korean War
and discusses its events and legacy.
  ISBN 1-56006-409-9
  1. Korean War, 1950-1953—Juvenile literature. 2. Korean War,
1950-1953—United States—Juvenile literature. [1. Korean War,
1950-1953.] I. Title. II. Series.
DS918.B24 1991
951.9—dc20   91-23065

Copyright 1991 by Lucent Books, Inc., P.O. Box 289011,
San Diego, CA 92198-0011
No part of this book may be reproduced or used in any other form or by
any other means, electrical, mechanical, or otherwise, including, but not
limited to photocopy, recording, or any information storage and retrieval
system, without prior written permission from the publisher.

Contents

Foreword

War, justifiable or not, is a descent into madness. George Washington, America's first president and commander-in-chief of its armed forces, wrote that his most fervent wish was "to see this plague of mankind, war, banished from the earth." Most, if not all of the forty presidents who succeeded Washington have echoed similar sentiments. Despite this, not one generation of Americans since the founding of the republic has been spared the maelstrom of war. In its brief history of just over two hundred years, the United States has been a combatant in eleven major wars. And four of those conflicts have occurred in the last fifty years.

America's reasons for going to war have differed little from those of most nations. Political, social, and economic forces were at work which either singly or in combination ushered America into each of its wars. A desire for independence motivated the Revolutionary War. The fear of annihilation led to the War of 1812. A related fear, that of having the nation divided, precipitated the Civil War. The need to contain an aggressor nation brought the United States into the Korean War. And territorial ambition lay behind the Mexican-American and the Indian Wars. Like all countries, America, at different times in its history, has been victimized by these forces and its citizens have been called to arms.

Whatever reasons may have been given to justify the use of military force, not all of America's wars have been popular. From the Revolutionary War to the Vietnam War, support of the people has alternately waxed and waned. For example, less than half of the colonists backed America's war of independence. In fact, most historians agree that at least one-third were committed to maintaining America's colonial status. During the Spanish-American War, a strong antiwar movement also developed. Resistance to the war was so high that the Democratic party made condemning the war a significant part of its platform in an attempt to lure voters into voting Democratic. The platform stated that "the burning issue of imperialism growing out of the Spanish war involves the very existence of the Republic and the destruction of our free institutions." More recently, the Vietnam War divided the nation like no other conflict had since the Civil War. The mushrooming antiwar movements in most major cities and colleges throughout the United States did more to bring that war to a conclusion than did actions on the battlefield.

Yet, there have been wars which have enjoyed overwhelming public support. World Wars I and II were popular because people believed that the survival of America's democratic institutions was at stake. In both wars, the American people rallied with an enthusiasm and spirit of self-sacrifice that was remarkable for a country with such a diverse population. Support for food and fuel rationing, the purchase of war bonds, a high rate of voluntary enlistments, and countless other forms of voluntarism, were characteristic of the people's response to those wars. Most recently, the Persian Gulf War prompted an unprecedented show of support even though the United States was not directly threatened by the conflict. Rallies in support of U.S. troops were widespread. Tens of thousands of individuals, including families, friends, and well-wishers of the troops sent packages of food, cosmetics, clothes, cassettes, and suntan oil. And even more supporters wrote letters to unknown soldiers that were forwarded to the military front. In fact, most public opinion polls revealed that up to 90 percent of all Americans approved of their nation's involvement.

The complex interplay of events and purposes that leads to military conflict should be included in a history of any war. A simple chronicling of battles and casualty lists at best offers only a partial history of war. Wars do not spontaneously erupt; nor does their memory perish. They are driven by underlying causes, fueled by policymakers, fought and supported by citizens, and remembered by those plotting a nation's future. For these reasons wars, or the fear of wars, will always leave an indelible stamp on any nation's history and influence its future.

The purpose of this series is to provide a full understanding of America's Wars by presenting each war in a historical context. Each of the twelve volumes focuses on the events that led up to the war, the war itself, its impact on the home front, and its aftermath and influence upon future conflicts. The unique personalities, the dramatic acts of courage and compassion, as well as the despair and horror of war are all presented in this series. Together, they show why America's wars have dominated American consciousness in the past as well as how they guide many political decisions of today. In these vivid and objective accounts, students will gain an understanding of why America became involved in these conflicts, and how historians, military and government officials, and others have come to understand and interpret that involvement.

Chronology of Events

1950

June 25 North Korean army invades South Korea.

June 27 United Nations Security Council calls on members to help South Korea repel the attack.

July 7 Gen. Douglas MacArthur appointed as head of the United Nations command.

September 15 Inchon landing.

October 3 China warns it will attack if U.S. troops cross the 38th parallel.

October 7 U.S. troops cross the 38th parallel.

October 14 Chinese army crosses Yalu River, moving south into North Korea.

October 24 MacArthur gives order that American forces are free to move to the Yalu River.

October 27 Chinese soldiers attack troops under the command of American general Walton Walker.

November 26 United Nations troops retreat.

1951

January 11 United Nations proposes a cease-fire agreement.

January 17 Cease-fire proposal is rejected by China.

February 1 United Nations declares China to be an aggressor state.

April 11 President Harry Truman fires Mac-Arthur, and Gen. Matthew Ridgway takes over command.

June 23 Soviets call for a cease-fire.

July 10 Armistice negotiations begin at Kaesong.

November 26 Demarcation line is established.

1952

January 8 Communists reject proposal that prisoners of war should be free to decide where to live after the war.

May 7 Both sides announce stalemate in the peace talks over issue of prisoners of war.

May 7 Gen. Francis T. Dodd is seized by prisoners of war at the prison camp on Koje Island.

May 12 Gen. Mark W. Clark succeeds General Ridgway as UN commander.

October 8 Peace talks go into recess.

November 4 Dwight D. Eisenhower wins presidential election.

1953

February 22 Exchange of sick and wounded prisoners proposed.

March 5 Joseph Stalin dies.

April 20 Sick and wounded prisoners are exchanged under Operation Little Switch.

April 26 Armistice talks resume at Panmunjom.

May 22 United States hints at future expansion of the war.

June 8 Prisoner-of-war question is resolved.

July 27 Armistice agreement is signed.

August 5 Full exchange of prisoners of war takes place under Operation Big Switch.

INTRODUCTION

The Korean Conflict

A visitor wandering through the statue- and monument-filled streets and avenues of Washington, D.C., today will find no national tribute in bronze or in stone to the heroes of the Korean War. Unlike the men and women who served in all other U.S. wars, the veterans of the Korean conflict have not been acknowledged by the United States.

Until the 1980s, the Korean conflict had been the forgotten war of American history. Korean veterans were not honored with military parades upon their return to the United States. Although many Korean veterans sustained horrible physical and mental wounds as a result of their experiences in Korea, these scars of war were not talked about in public and received little attention. Similarly, history textbooks made little or no reference to the war in Korea.

This lack of interest reflected a national desire to forget the events of the war as quickly as possible. It had been a long, difficult, and bloody war in which the United States sustained more than 140,000 casualties, including more than 33,000 killed in action. The war had been fought on inhospitable Asian battlefields. It had been fought against an enemy that was not as well armed as the American troops but that was prepared to fight ferociously. Enemy troops were willing to sustain huge losses of their own soldiers and the virtual destruction of their country. These North Korean soldiers were fanatically dedicated to the principles of communism. American troops found it difficult to understand such political and ideological zeal, but they soon discovered that this political conviction made enemy soldiers difficult to defeat on the battlefield.

A wounded U.S. Marine during the Korean conflict.

Mistakes and Miscalculations

American military and political leaders made many mistakes and miscalculations in the war, which contributed to its unpopularity. They misjudged the number of soldiers and weapons required to win the conflict. They also misjudged the aggressiveness of the North Koreans. These leaders lulled themselves into thinking that China would not come to the assistance of the North Koreans. They did not understand that China would never permit the presence of enemy forces along its border with Korea.

The Americans fooled themselves into believing that the leaders and the military forces of South Korea were prepared to defend their newly achieved independence. They misjudged the ability and the willingness of the South Korean peasants to mount a successful and sustained military campaign. They failed to understand the intricacies of the relationship among North Korea, China, and the Soviet Union and were never certain with whom they were at war. But above all, the government and military leaders of the United States forgot one of the major lessons of World War II. That lesson was never again to commit American troops to fighting an Asian war on Asian battlefields.

No wonder the American people, the war veterans, and the country's military and civilian leaders wanted to forget about the Korean War as quickly as possible. And because they did forget, they failed to acknowledge and then to learn from their mistakes.

Korea and Vietnam

As a result, in 1953, the year the Korean War ended, American leaders began taking steps to lead American troops into an eerily similar conflict in Vietnam. The outcome of this war in Vietnam might have been quite different if U.S. leaders and the American people had not been so willing to forget the Korean War. And, in essence, it is important to remember this forgotten war, and all wars, so that American lives will never have to be wasted to learn a painful lesson twice.

CHAPTER ONE

Why Korea? Why the United States? Why the United Nations?

On Saturday evening, June 24, 1950, the American secretary of state, Dean Acheson, placed an urgent telephone call to Harry Truman, the president of the United States. Truman, on vacation, was relaxing in his home in Independence, Missouri, after a leisurely family dinner. He picked up the telephone, listened for a few moments, and then knew that the course of American history had changed.

Acheson informed the president that North Korean forces had begun a well-organized and many-pronged invasion of South Korea, a country whose independence the United States was obligated to defend. Truman believed the action held great significance for the United States. He believed that the North Koreans would not have acted on their own without prompting by the Soviet Union. For Truman, the Korean invasion meant that the Soviet Union was directly challenging the United States. The president accepted the challenge. He told one aide: "By God, I'm going to let them have it."

Since the end of World War II, the United States and the Soviet Union had engaged in a seemingly endless series of disagreements all over the world. These disagreements reflected the political, economic, and social differences between the two countries. Both countries viewed each world conflict as part of their rivalry. Each wanted to have the support and backing of as many other countries as possible.

Since the two countries had not yet come into armed conflict over their differences, the rivalry between the Soviet Union and the United States was known as the Cold War. Communist North

145928

Korea's invasion of South Korea altered this Cold War situation. Truman believed that if the United States failed to respond to the invasion, it could lead the Soviet Union directly to attack the United States and its allies.

In his *Memoirs,* Truman describes his state of mind upon hearing of the invasion of South Korea:

> In my generation, this was not the first occasion when the strong had attacked the weak. I recalled some earlier instances; Manchuria, Ethiopia, and Austria. I remembered how each time that the democracies failed to act it had encouraged the aggressors to keep going ahead. Communism was acting in Korea just as Hitler, Mussolini and the Japanese had acted. I felt certain that if South Korea was allowed to go unchallenged it would mean a third world war.

In 1950, the Soviet Union was powerful enough to challenge the United States all over the world. Truman and much of the American public believed the United States had a duty to oppose the Soviet Union everywhere it could, through force if necessary.

The independence of South Korea was significant to the United States not only because of the conflict with the Soviet Union. Keeping South Korea free was also important because Korea was close to Japan, where a large number of American troops were stationed.

Korea's History

This strategic location as well as the history of Korea help to explain why the United States became involved in a civil war between the people of North and South Korea. Korea is a peninsula lying at the southern tip of the Asian continent. It is a small nation, approximately the size of England and Scotland combined. It is surrounded on the east by the Sea of Japan, on the west by the China Sea, on most of its northern border by the Chinese province of Manchuria, and at the most easterly tip of its northern border by the Soviet Union.

Although Americans knew little about Korea in the nineteenth century, Korea's three powerful neighbors—China, Japan, and the Soviet Union—were very interested in the strategically located little country. Each country wanted to control Korea to protect its own borders. None of these three nations wanted to see Korea fall to the others.

For hundreds of years, Korea was dominated by China and served as the southern border of that great, sprawling empire. But by the end of the nineteenth century, the Chinese empire had lost much of its military power. China's powerful neighbors conquered parts of China. During World War II, Japan controlled Korea and used that country's natural resources.

Toward the end of World War II, Japan still had large numbers of soldiers stationed in Korea. During the war, the United States and the Soviet Union cooperated to defeat the Japanese in Korea. The Soviet Union from the north and the United States from the south invaded Korea and defeated Japanese troops stationed in that country.

The United States and the Soviet Union agreed to divide Korea along a line of latitude, called the 38th parallel, for wartime military and administrative purposes. The Soviet Union occupied the north, and the United States occupied the south. The division and occupation were to be temporary. Both countries agreed to withdraw from Korea and relinquish their control to a Korean leader at the end of the war.

Unfortunately, cooperation between the United States and the Soviet Union ended with World War II. Instead of withdrawing occupation forces, the United States and the Soviet Union became more deeply involved in Korea.

The United States wanted Korea to be unified under a democratic government with regularly held elections. The United States hoped that such a government would be friendly to American interests. The Soviet Union, on the other hand, wanted Korea to be unified under a communist form of government. The Soviets hoped such a government would be tied to the Soviet Union and would serve as a stepping-stone to further Soviet conquests in Southeast Asia.

The two powers could not resolve their differences. As a result, final arrangements for Korea were never made, and it remained divided. Given this impasse, the United States decided to bring the Korean problem before the United Nations.

The United Nations

The United Nations (UN) had been formed during World War II. Its founders hoped it would help member nations cooperate to resolve international problems peacefully. The United States very eagerly, and the Soviet Union reluctantly, supported the work of the United Nations.

The UN agreed to sponsor and to oversee national elections in Korea. The UN hoped these elections would result in a national assembly that could begin to restore peace and prosperity to Korea.

A United Nations Temporary Commission on Korea was established in Seoul, the capital of Korea to oversee the elections. The commission began its work on January 12, 1948. Unfortunately, the commission members were not permitted to enter North Korea to oversee elections there. Separate elections were held in the north and in the south.

The Cold War

The Cold War refers to the ideological war between the United States and the Soviet Union following World War II. Although the countries cooperated during the war to destroy Nazi Germany and totalitarian Japan, the differences in their ideas and values resurfaced after the war. After 1945, the United States and its European allies were angry and confused as the Soviet Union seized control of the countries of eastern and central Europe. In each of these countries, the Soviet Union brutally suppressed all who opposed communism or Soviet domination.

People in the United States came to believe that they had fought to destroy the evil of Nazism only to see it replaced by the equally evil system of communism.

Because both sides possessed atomic weapons, which could result in total destruction, the United States and the Soviet Union could not settle their differences through war. Instead, each side looked for opportunities to win small economic, political, or military victories, often by using other countries to fight their battles.

The Cold War remained the dominant force in world politics until the collapse of communism in the Soviet Union. For the first time since 1945, the Cold War has ceased.

The United Nations

The United Nations was established at the end of World War II. Its creation was the fulfillment of the dream of President Franklin Roosevelt and of the leaders of many other nations. These men wanted to create an international organization formed of all independent countries to prevent another world war.

The desire for such an organization was so strong that Roosevelt, Prime Minister Winston Churchill of Great Britain, and Soviet leader Joseph Stalin even discussed the idea of a United Nations organization during their wartime meetings to defeat Nazi Germany.

In 1944, a major planning conference was held at Dumbarton Oaks near Washington, D.C. At Dumbarton Oaks, world representatives began working out details regarding the organization of the United Nations. Then, in the spring of 1945, an additional international meeting was held in San Francisco. A draft charter for the United Nations received approval at the San Francisco meeting. Those nations at war with Germany participated in the final design of the new world organization.

All peace-loving nations were invited to become part of the UN General Assembly. These nations would work together to make the assembly a kind of world forum for discussion of international issues. The General Assembly, however, was too large a group to act quickly if an international crisis developed. Therefore, the framers of the United Nations charter also created a smaller body called the Security Council. The Security Council consisted of eleven members. Five of these—the United States, Great Britain, France, China, and the Soviet Union—held permanent seats and had the right to veto any resolution. Six other members were elected on a rotating basis.

The United Nations was given authority to form its own general staff and to call upon member nations to contribute troops in times of international necessity. Yet, despite the design of the United Nations and the authority granted to it, many world leaders remained skeptical of its ability to protect the independence of one nation attacked by another.

These skeptics remembered that the predecessor of the United Nations, the League of Nations, had been a weak international organization. It had been unable to stop the aggressions of the 1930s that led to World War II.

The Korean War proved to be the testing ground for the United Nations. The conflict provided an opportunity to demonstrate whether a world organization could actually take up arms in the defense of weak nations threatened by aggression.

American occupation forces withdraw from South Korea at the end of 1949.

As a result of the elections in South Korea, a seventy-four-year-old, American-educated Korean nationalist named Dr. Syngman Rhee was elected president. He established a democratic government with a national legislature. In hopes that North Koreans would join the assembly, Rhee left one hundred seats vacant.

Meanwhile, a separate, Soviet-sponsored, one-party election took place in the north. It resulted in the establishment of a communist dictatorship under the direction of a young, Soviet-trained Korean nationalist named Kim Il Sung. After the establishment of this government at Panmunjom, the Soviets withdrew in December 1948. They left behind a large, well-trained, and well-equipped North Korean army with Soviet advisers, airplanes, and 150 Soviet-built T-34 tanks to back up the communist regime.

In response to the elections in North Korea, the United States promised to build up the army of South Korea to protect the newly established democracy against its northern neighbor. But the United States feared that fiercely nationalistic Syngman Rhee would use American military hardware to unify his country by force once the Americans left.

To counter this threat, the United States left the South Korean army a small array of American light arms and advisers. These advisers trained an eight-division South Korean army. At the end of 1949, American occupation forces left South Korea.

From 1948 to 1950, the 38th parallel was the scene of frequent, short skirmishes between the two Korean armies. Each

Communism

Communism is an economic theory dealing with the ownership of property and the distribution of goods. Communists believe that all property should be owned collectively by society. They believe that each individual should work for the good of the society. In return, society gives individuals everything they need to live.

These ideas were first expressed by Karl Marx (1818–1883) and Friedrich Engels (1820–1895). These men theorized that communism would first develop in the economically advanced societies of western Europe, where there were enough goods and services to provide for the needs of everyone. Instead, communism first appeared in economically backward Russia after the revolution of 1917. Communism was forced upon the Russian government by a small group of determined believers. These men ruthlessly suppressed all opposition groups and imposed communism on their society through state regulation and control of all sectors of the economy. Soviet leaders believed communism had to be enforced quickly and through force to increase the country's productivity.

Communist leaders saw Western democracies as the eternal enemy.

side tested the military strength of the other. These skirmishes were paralleled by confrontations between the United States and the Soviet Union in Greece, Turkey, and Czechoslovakia. Each side tested the other's willingness to protect its turf through military force. The Cold War appeared to encompass the entire globe.

An Ideological Battle

During these years, both countries viewed all international confrontations in terms of gains or losses in the Cold War. Any diplomatic or economic gain for the United States was viewed as a defeat by the Soviet Union. Any government that turned communist or any Communist party in any country that won an election was regarded as a victory for the Soviet Union.

That was why Harry Truman reacted so strongly to the news of the North Korean invasion of South Korea. The Cold War atmosphere also helps to explain why he decided to involve the United Nations in the Korean conflict.

The United States had played a crucial role in creating the United Nations. If the UN were successful in restoring peace between the two Korean countries, it would be an enormous victory for the young world organization. It would also be a victory for the United States, which had helped to create it. Therefore, Truman felt certain that the UN should play a major role in defending South Korea against the attack.

UN ambassador Warren R. Austin urged the UN Security Council to aid South Korea in its struggle against North Korea.

Gen. Douglas MacArthur (left) was commander in chief of all UN forces in Korea. America's entry into the conflict caused thousands of American soldiers to say good-bye to their loved ones (right).

Harry Truman instructed his ambassador to the UN, Warren R. Austin, to urge the Security Council of the United Nations to come to the support of South Korea.

In 1950, the UN was very much influenced by Western, and mainly American, opinion. So it is not surprising that when Ambassador Austin presented the American position to the Security Council, the vote on Sunday, June 25, 1950, supported the United States. The Security Council voted that North Korea had violated international peace agreements and ordered its armies to withdraw across the 38th parallel.

President Harry S Truman ordered General MacArthur to send two American divisions to Korea.

But withdrawal did not occur. In response, on June 27, the United Nations Security Council called on all members of the organization to "furnish such assistance to the Republic of Korea as may be necessary to repel the armed attack and to restore international peace and security in the area."

The Soviet Union was boycotting the United Nations when the Security Council took these momentous votes. The Security Council could therefore give unanimous backing to an armed, international action against North Korea.

The stand taken by the Security Council was extraordinary. As Dean Acheson wrote, "For the first time in world history international aggression was countered according to a code of collective security." The decision of the Security Council gave the

Soviet Walkout

In May 1950, the Soviet delegate to the United Nations, Jacob Malik, stopped attending UN meetings. His behavior was prompted by a controversy over China.

China had been awarded a permanent seat on the United Nations Security Council after World War II. In 1949, communist Chinese rebels toppled the government of Gen. Chiang Kai-shek. Chiang and his followers escaped from mainland China and set up a government on the island of Formosa.

The United States had been General Chiang's longest and closest friend. Americans were outraged that the communists had taken over China and demanded that the U.S. government continue to send support to Formosa. Such support included the continued recognition of Chiang Kai-shek as the leader of China and the legitimate holder of China's permanent seat on the United Nations Security Council.

The Soviets disagreed with this decision and staunchly supported the interests of communist China. They urged that communist China receive the permanent seat in the UN and the veto power that accompanied it. The United Nations refused to grant these demands, and Jacob Malik expressed his government's dissatisfaction by refusing to attend sessions of the United Nations.

The Soviet walkout was one of the most dramatic events in the history of the UN. By walking out, the Soviets gave up all power to veto resolutions they disliked. In June 1950, during the Soviet ambassador's absence, the Security Council considered what to do about the North Korean invasion of South Korea. Because the Soviet ambassador was not present, the Security Council was able to vote in favor of military support for South Korea. In order to prevent a similar incident, the Soviet Union has never again boycotted sessions of the Security Council.

Jacob Malik (in hat) talks with newsmen after leading his delegation out of the UN Security Council.

world hope that the United Nations would effectively maintain international peace.

The United States Enters the Conflict

Following the Security Council decision, Truman ordered Gen. Douglas MacArthur, commander in chief of American forces in Japan, to send two American divisions to assist South Korea immediately. Because of the major role the United States would play in the conflict, the United Nations on July 8, 1950, named General MacArthur commander in chief of all UN forces in Korea. Although the conflict continued as a UN action, the organization thereafter generally left the direction of the war to President Truman, the American Joint Chiefs of Staff, and to MacArthur.

These UN forces included soldiers from many countries. President Syngman Rhee even placed his own South Korean army under MacArthur's command. When complete, that command came to include the South Korean army; six American divisions (five army and one marine); a British division drawn from Great Britain, Canada, Australia, and New Zealand; a Turkish brigade; and battalions from France, the Netherlands, Greece, Belgium, and the Philippines. Thailand, Colombia, and India sent medical units to assist the UN army.

At home, Truman requested a major overhaul of the American armed forces. Congress prepared to vote for huge increases in military expenditures. This money would create a more powerful and modern army to support the UN military action. The fate of South Korea now rested in the hands of those who were willing to defend it.

CHAPTER TWO

The North Korean Phase

A great deal was at stake for South Korea and the United States in stopping the North Korean invasion. If the invasion were successful, all of Korea would be unified by the communists under Kim Il Sung. The defeat of South Korea would be a grave humiliation for its democratic government. In addition, it would be a terrible Cold War setback for the United States and the United Nations. Perhaps most horrible of all, if typical of other communist invasions, upon taking over, the North Koreans would kill or imprison anyone who had supported the democratic leaders or government.

Even with so much at stake, the early days of the war did not go well for the UN forces. The 38th parallel was only lightly manned by South Korean units that were not as strong as the enemy troops. The democratic Republic of Korea forces, called the ROK, were entirely unprepared for attack. They had not been properly alerted, and they were not ready for battle. In fact, when the first attack came, only one rifle company was stationed at the 38th parallel to face the heavily armed North Korean People's Army, or NKPA.

The entire American command was also taken by surprise. Gen. Charles A. Willoughby, MacArthur's intelligence officer, had told his chief in March 1950 that "there will be no civil war in Korea this spring or summer." Even though President Syngman Rhee of South Korea believed otherwise, his fears were dismissed because he had warned of invasion plans so often in the past. When the attack did come, only one U.S. Army officer, thirty-year-old Capt. Joseph R. Darrigo, witnessed the arrival of the North Koreans at Kaesong, the ancient Korean capital.

Syngman Rhee

Syngman Rhee (1875–1965) was a Korean patriot and anticommunist who had early and openly opposed Japanese domination of Korea. In 1904, Rhee went to the United States where he became a champion of and spokesperson for Korean independence. He returned to his homeland in 1918 and took part in a national independence movement against the Japanese in 1919 that the Japanese brutally suppressed.

As part of their efforts to control Korean nationalism, the Japanese recruited dissatisfied Koreans to participate in the administration of Korea. Rhee viewed these Koreans with contempt—they were willing to collaborate with the Japanese conquerors of Korea in exchange for an easier life. Rhee himself escaped to Shanghai, where in 1921 he helped to establish a Korean Provisional Government (KPG) in exile. He later spent the years of World War II in the United States, where he was a constant and persistent advocate for recognition of the KPG as the legitimate government of Korea.

After World War II, the United States wanted a strong Korean leader to form a democratic government and unify the country. Syngman Rhee's long and outspoken advocacy of Korean interests made him the natural choice of Americans anxious to leave Korea in the hands of Koreans.

Unfortunately, Syngman Rhee was an authoritarian leader who had many old scores to settle. He often used his military forces more harshly against internal opposition than he did against the armies of North Korea. Rhee also frequently interfered with the strategic plans of the UN commanders. In particular, he refused to accept the idea of a permanently divided Korea. In the end, the United Nations had as many difficulties with Syngman Rhee as it did with Kim Il Sung in achieving an end to the Korean conflict.

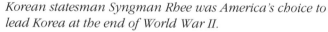

Korean statesman Syngman Rhee was America's choice to lead Korea at the end of World War II.

American troops, armaments, and supplies were sent to South Korea.

Darrigo jumped into his jeep, driving wildly through the night, to spread the news of the attack. While Darrigo tried to rouse the ROK command at headquarters, the NKPA continued its combined land and sea operation. They attacked the ROK units both from the front and the flanks. The force of these attacks compelled ROK troops all along the border to retreat and regroup behind the 38th parallel. During the retreat, several units of the ROK were completely overrun and destroyed.

The defeated ROK soldiers withdrew first to Uijongbu, and then across the Imjin River to Seoul, the capital of South Korea. The NKPA kept driving south. Soon, both Seoul and the nearby Kimpo airport, located about fifty miles south of the 38th parallel, were in danger of being overrun by the North Korean forces.

At this point, the ROK command committed a terrible mistake. Instead of attempting to stall the enemy advance in the north, the troops thought only of escape. The ROK hoped to delay the enemy by blowing up the bridges across the Han River, which lies to the south of Seoul. Tragically, if the ROK did blow up the bridges, thousands of South Korean soldiers would be trapped north of Seoul and in the city itself.

The Bridges Are Destroyed

American advisers in Seoul begged the South Korean generals to wait until the last possible moment before blowing up the bridges. Somehow, the orders did not reach the proper authorities. On June 28, an enormous explosion shook Seoul as the bridges were blown up and fell into the river. Hundreds of people were on the bridges and fell to their deaths in the river below. Many thousands of South Korean soldiers were isolated north of the river. Many of them were captured by the advancing North Korean army. Remaining South Korean units disintegrated. The pitiful remnants of the ROK, perhaps only twenty-five thousand of its original ninety-eight thousand, retreated south to the town of Taejon. The North Korean army seemed destined to sweep through South Korea and take the entire country.

Troop reinforcements were desperately needed to stop the advance of the North Korean army. MacArthur sent an urgent message to Truman. More troops must be sent immediately to South Korea or all would be lost.

The problem was that there were few troops available. After World War II, the United States had greatly reduced the size of its army and the expensive support systems that keep a modern army ready to fight. The United States had only a few full-strength divisions, and these were stationed in Europe, not the Far East.

The only troops the United States could immediately spare to meet the initial crisis of the Korean conflict were two poorly trained, unseasoned units that had been stationed in Japan. They arrived in South Korea in mid-July. They were not able to withstand the NKPA assault any better than the South Korean units.

These poorly prepared American soldiers were badly mauled by the North Korean army, which continued to inflict heavy casualties on the American and ROK troops. But, assisted in part by the planes of the Australian and American air forces, the Americans temporarily held their ground in Taejon. President Syngman Rhee, who had fled from Seoul on June 27, set up his temporary government headquarters at Taejon because of its relative safety and the presence of an airport. There, the South Korean president tried to rally his soldiers.

The American and ROK troops and small units from other countries were now organized as UN forces. They succeeded in delaying the advance of North Korean forces for five days, from July 16 to July 21, at Taejon. Those five days were crucial. They helped to prevent the NKPA from completely overrunning South Korea. During that time, two more UN divisions landed at the South Korean port of Pusan and built a defensive position north of the port. By July 27, this position was strong enough to prevent the NKPA from driving the UN forces into the Sea of Japan.

American troops arrive at the port of Pusan.

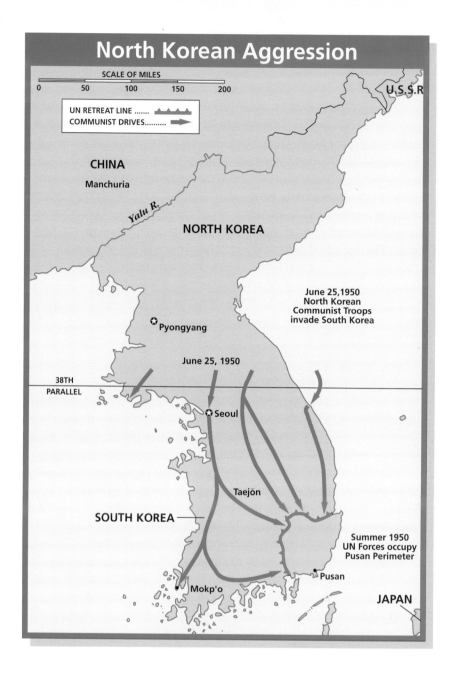

North Korean Aggression

SCALE OF MILES

0   50   100   150   200

UN RETREAT LINE ....

COMMUNIST DRIVES..........

U.S.S.R

CHINA

Manchuria

Yalu R.

NORTH KOREA

June 25,1950
North Korean
Communist Troops
invade South Korea

✪ Pyongyang

June 25, 1950

38TH
PARALLEL

✪ Seoul

Taejŏn

SOUTH KOREA

Summer 1950
UN Forces occupy
Pusan Perimeter

● Pusan

● Mokp'o

JAPAN

The port of Pusan was also made secure enough to receive badly needed additional troops and supplies.

By early August 1950, the tide of the North Korean attack was slowed. During the next two months, many more troops arrived. But unless some other strategy were employed, the North Koreans would soon resume their attack against Pusan and its defenders. South Korea was still in danger of falling to the powerful North Korean army.

This was one of the darkest moments of the conflict. UN forces anticipated a renewed attack before adequate reinforcements could reach them through Pusan. Many feared the UN

"Gook Syndrome"

The American people were very satisfied with themselves when the Korean War began. Many believed that Americans produced the best of everything and because of their victory in World War II had earned the right to dominate less industrially developed nations. Unfortunately, many Americans had no appreciation of the differences among cultures and had no understanding of people who were not American.

These views were especially strong among the American soldiers who fought in the Korean War. Many of these soldiers had not been able to fit into traditional American society and so had joined the army. Now, they found themselves in an Asian country that they did not understand.

Many of these young men exhibited what the military establishment called the "gook syndrome." These soldiers considered the Koreans and Chinese to be inferior people and believed they could be pushed aside and discounted. The soldiers called the Asians "gooks," a derogatory name. The United States also considered the Korean military to be inferior to the American army.

The American soldiers discounted the fighting ability of the North Koreans and the Chinese, which led to carelessness and almost disaster. American armies were overrun and almost destroyed on several occasions by North Korean and Chinese forces which were less well-armed, less well-fed, and less well-clothed.

This "gook syndrome" was shared by soldiers and officers alike. Indeed, the soldiers may have picked up many of their prejudices from the officers who led them. Gen. George Barth, for example, could not hide his contempt for the Asian enemy. He arrived with the first troops from Japan, the Twenty-fourth Division. On July 5, 1950, Barth told a news reporter, "The Commie bastards will turn and run when they're up against our boys. We'll be back in Seoul again by the weekend." He concluded his remarks by adding that he and his troops were "going to kick some gooks and get out."

troops were too weak to hold on and would have to evacuate Korea entirely.

"I Can Handle Them"

Douglas MacArthur, directing the UN forces, was determined not to let South Korea fall to North Korea. Supremely confident of his own abilities, he announced, "If Washington will not hobble me, I can handle them [the North Koreans] with one hand tied behind my back." MacArthur, like many other Americans in Southeast Asia, was a victim of the "gook syndrome," which led him to believe that in all things, Americans were superior to Asians.

The general set out to prove the truth of his boast. He conceived a brilliant but farfetched plan to prevent the destruction of South Korea. He decided to land a UN army far to the north, behind the North Korean army concentrated around Pusan. If successful, MacArthur would take the pressure off the desperate ROK and American forces trapped at Pusan. His army could then cut off the retreat of the North Korean armies in the south and destroy them before they could escape back across the 38th parallel.

MacArthur's plan was given the secret code name Operation Chromite. The area in the north where the UN troops were to land was the port of Inchon. Inchon is on the west coast of Korea, just a few miles west of Seoul and about one hundred miles north of where nearly 100,000 North Korean forces were located.

All indications were that such a mission would be a failure. The approaches to Inchon Harbor are treacherous. There are huge tidal changes, underwater islands in the approach channels, and enormous mud flats that can strand boats and men. In addition, the North Koreans had heavy guns placed on Wolmi-do Island in the mouth of the harbor. These, in turn, defended the high walls that guarded Inchon Harbor itself. According to Gen. Matthew B. Ridgway, Operation Chromite was a "five thousand to one gamble," and military leaders in Washington only reluctantly gave their consent to the plan.

Operation Chromite would be a truly international undertaking. Troops from Britain, Australia, New Zealand, Canada, and the Netherlands joined the Americans and South Koreans. The Inchon landing was massive. It required great attention to detail in its planning stages. More than two hundred ships and countless planes were to take part in the daring operation.

An Insane Plan

MacArthur's most difficult task was to convince the navy and marines that his plan would work. The chiefs of the navy and marines balked at the thought of landing men in possible thirty-five-foot tides. They had to develop special equipment for

UN troops land at Inchon.

American troops and equipment land ashore at Inchon.

defusing mines that they believed were in the harbor. They would also need special scaling ladders to climb the high walls protecting the harbor. Elaborate equipment was required for the advance parties of marines who would have to be landed first and would hold the sea approaches until the actual fighting troops arrived.

Miraculously, all went as scheduled. The guns guarding the harbor were destroyed, and the first assault forces landed with few casualties. They captured the high ground overlooking the city and also the railroad line and main highway between Seoul and Inchon. Once these were captured, enemy troops were prevented from entering or leaving Inchon. When the main attack began, the sky over Inchon was literally darkened by the huge number of aircraft that protected the assaulting forces and stopped possible enemy troops from interfering with the invasion from the land side of the harbor.

One journalist observing the landing wrote, "It possessed the drama and excitement of great assemblages of men and means brought together to carry out huge common purposes."

Only sixteen hundred North Koreans were stationed in Inchon to oppose the UN force of more than seventy thousand. Clearly, such a small force could do little to prevent the UN forces from taking Inchon. With Inchon secured, U.S. Marines raced for the Kimpo airport, which was also lightly guarded. It fell quickly to the UN troops.

September 15, 1950, turned out to be a spectacularly successful day for the UN forces. By day's end, the well-equipped and well-trained assault forces had overcome all obstacles in the harbor and had completed one of the most successful amphibious, or combined land and sea, operations in history.

With the port and the airport secured, UN troops continued on to Seoul. They wanted to regain the city before the NKPA could send massive reinforcements. The attack on Seoul began on September 22, 1950. At first, the UN forces attacked on a narrow front that permitted the NKPA to concentrate machine guns and artillery on the attackers. There were gruesome exchanges among the NKPA, UN forces, and American Corsair airplanes helping to destroy the enemy.

UN forces then proceeded to approach the city from many fronts, which prevented the small North Korean force of eight thousand from concentrating its artillery in any one place. By September 26, the city was sealed off, and the fight for Seoul was fought from street to street with high casualties on both sides. Seoul fell to the UN troops on September 27. On September 29, General MacArthur led President Syngman Rhee back into the capital city.

The Benefits of Inchon

The Inchon landing was an enormous gamble and an enormous success for MacArthur. Not only was Seoul regained but, more important, MacArthur established the UN force in a powerful strategic position. It was far to the north of the majority of the 100,000 North Koreans who were now cut off from safety. All MacArthur had to do was capture that army and the war would be over.

The Inchon landing was the high point of MacArthur's career. The Joint Chiefs of Staff in Washington were astounded by his

An abandoned child after the fighting at Inchon (left). General MacArthur and aides observe the shelling at Inchon.

UN troops retake Seoul in September 1950.

uncanny insight and understanding of the enemy, who had continued to be drawn toward Pusan in the south for the final kill. The American people love a successful general, and MacArthur became one of their favorites.

MacArthur's success at Inchon made it difficult for the Joint Chiefs to challenge his decisions in the future. Unfortunately, after September 15, 1950, MacArthur made a series of extraordinarily unwise decisions.

One of these unfortunate decisions came immediately after the Inchon landing. MacArthur wanted to destroy the North Korean army still in the south. North Korean generals withheld news of the Inchon landing because they wanted the NKPA to keep up the attack against Pusan. But when the news could be concealed no longer, the army desperately tried to escape north.

All MacArthur had to do to prevent the escape was to send UN troops east across the Korean peninsula and cut off all escape routes. Instead, the general decided to put American troops at Inchon on ships, transport them by sea around the southern coast of Korea, and land them at the east coast port of Wonsan.

But the port of Wonsan was heavily mined, and the UN forces were not able to land as quickly as MacArthur had hoped. The troops were unable to stop many of the veteran North Korean soldiers from escaping. Perhaps as many as thirty thousand North Korean soldiers managed to escape through the mountain passes.

Despite this setback, the United Nations had achieved its initial goal. By the end of September 1950, UN forces had reached the 38th parallel and had reestablished South Korean independence.

Kim Il Sung

Kim Il Sung (1912–   ) was the leader of North Korea during the Korean War. He was a young, fanatic Korean nationalist who harassed Japanese troops in Manchuria and North Korea during the 1930s. His military and guerrilla talents were recognized by the Chinese communists who recruited him to continue his fight against the Japanese during World War II. He led roving bands of irregular soldiers against Japanese troops in many hit-and-run attacks that infuriated the Japanese.

Kim Il Sung attended military school in Moscow, fought at the battle of Stalingrad during World War II with the Soviet army, and returned to Korea as a major in the Soviet occupation forces.

Kim Il Sung's dedication to communism made him the ideal choice to lead North Korea, according to the Soviet Union and communist China. When the United States established a democratic form of government in the south, the Soviets created a communist government in the north and placed Kim Il Sung in charge. When Soviet troops withdrew from North Korea in 1948, they left huge stocks of ammunition and the powerful T-34 tanks. These weapons were used by the North Koreans against the UN forces in the early stages of the Korean War.

After the successful UN landing in Inchon, Kim Il Sung's North Korean army was forced to withdraw from South Korea. With the entry of communist China into the conflict, Kim Il Sung's role diminished, since his troops constituted only a small portion of the army fighting the UN armies.

Although North Korea suffered a loss of land as a result of the conflict, Kim Il Sung saw himself as a national hero. After the war, he called himself "the all-triumphant, resolute and incomparable commander and outstanding military strategist."

North Korean president Kim Il Sung, reviewing Chinese troops in 1987, led North Korea against South Korea.

Bombs destroy a dock warehouse at Wonsan (left). (Above) UN secretary general Trygve Lie (left), talks with U.S. general Mark Clark. Lie wanted the United States to unify Korea.

UN Goals Change

Now, however, the objective of the war changed. In June 1950, the independence of South Korea had been at stake. But back in 1948, the United Nations had wanted to oversee elections to unite the country. In September 1950, the UN desire to unify Korea reemerged. The goal was strongly supported by the United States as well.

Through their friends in the United Nations, the Chinese communists issued a public warning to the United States against an American advance north of the 38th parallel. The UN secretary general, Trygve Lie, however, believed that the United States had no choice but to act on behalf of the United Nations' intention to unify Korea. Lie therefore declared that the United Nations had "no alternative to an advance north of the 38th parallel." On October 7, 1950, the United Nations General Assembly adopted an American-sponsored resolution stating that it wished to see "a unified, independent, democratic Korea be established."

MacArthur's Limitations

With the sanction of the United Nations, the American Joint Chiefs of Staff directed General MacArthur to proceed north across the 38th parallel. The general was not given a completely free hand, however. There was some fear that either China or the Soviet Union might enter the conflict, an event that all concerned wished to avoid. Therefore, MacArthur's instructions contained limitations. He could move north of the 38th parallel and try to destroy the North Korean army with the objective of unifying Korea. But these instructions should not be followed if MacArthur's forces encountered Soviet or Chinese troops.

Chiang Kai-shek

Chiang Kai-shek (1887–1975) was a follower of the great Chinese leader Dr. Sun Yat-sen. When Sun died in 1925, Chiang took his place as the leader of the nationalist political party, known as the Kuomintang party. Chiang led his armies across China, uniting the country after many years of civil war, which had broken out after the overthrow of the last Chinese emperor.

Chiang was extremely arrogant. He failed to bring about the democratic reforms he had promised his people, and eventually, he alienated the vast majority of Chinese peasants who wanted land reform. Chiang also alienated communist and other left-wing reformers whom he threw out of the Kuomintang party. In part, he did this as part of deals he was forced to make with local influential men known as warlords who controlled not only powerful local armies but also the production of food in their regions. The communists charged that Chiang became rich as a result of these deals.

Initially, Chiang was looked upon sympathetically by the West during World War II because of China's invasion by Japanese troops and because of the atrocities committed there by Japanese soldiers. But Chiang lost that support because of his military ineptitude and his inability to improve the lives of his people.

The Chinese Communist party took advantage of Chiang's failure and gradually gained the support of the Chinese peasants. In 1949, Chiang was defeated by a powerful Communist army and fled with the remains of his own forces to the island of Formosa, which lies one hundred miles off the coast of China.

From time to time during the Korean War, American military leaders considered including Chiang's armies in the UN forces. But there was fear among many Americans that Chiang would take the opportunity to attempt to reconquer China, which would drag the United States into an unwanted and dangerous war with China.

Chiang Kai-shek led China for over twenty years. In 1949, he was ousted by the powerful Communist army.

General MacArthur and President Truman meet at Wake Island on October 15, 1950.

MacArthur was told not to cross the Manchurian border that separated North Korea from communist China. He was denied permission to use Chiang Kai-shek's Chinese troops on Formosa because this act would anger the Chinese communists. He was to use only South Korean troops, not American soldiers or marines, near the Manchurian border in order to avoid Chinese fears of an American invasion of China.

President Truman felt uneasy about MacArthur's willingness to observe these limitations. He feared that MacArthur might ignore his instructions and press on even if he did encounter Chinese troops. This fear was prompted by the fact that MacArthur had publicly announced that he did not agree with the UN objectives.

So on October 15, 1950, Truman flew to Wake Island in the Pacific Ocean to meet with MacArthur. Neither man looked forward to the encounter. On the way to the Wake Island meeting, the president wrote to a family member that he was off to "talk to God's right hand man." Before leaving Tokyo, the general made reference to "the damned State Department, Truman and Communists." MacArthur would remain on guard against the evil people in control.

At Wake Island, Truman emphasized that the United Nations had only limited objectives, namely, the liberation of Korea and, if possible, the establishment of a democratic government under Syngman Rhee. MacArthur assured the president that he intended to carefully follow these instructions. The general told the president he did not expect the Chinese to intervene.

MacArthur told Truman that at most, the Chinese could put sixty thousand troops into the field and that the UN forces could

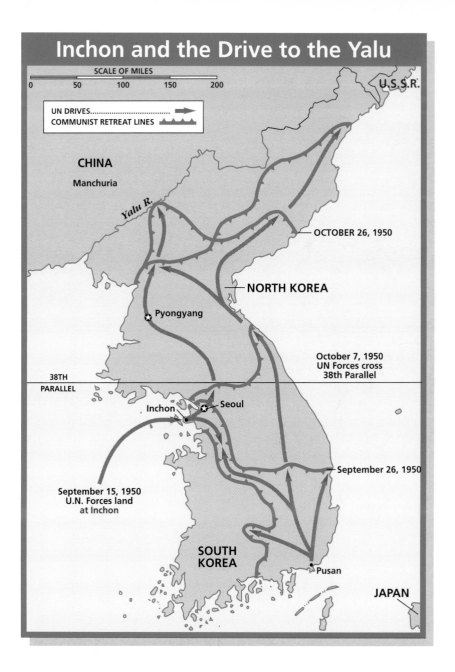

Inchon and the Drive to the Yalu

SCALE OF MILES

0   50   100   150   200

UN DRIVES..............................
COMMUNIST RETREAT LINES

U.S.S.R.

CHINA

Manchuria

Yalu R.

OCTOBER 26, 1950

NORTH KOREA

Pyongyang

October 7, 1950
UN Forces cross
38th Parallel

38TH
PARALLEL

Inchon   Seoul

September 26, 1950

September 15, 1950
U.N. Forces land
at Inchon

SOUTH
KOREA

Pusan

JAPAN

destroy such a force as soon as it crossed the Yalu River and
entered Korea. General MacArthur also told Truman that he
anticipated his operation would be completed by Thanksgiving
and that American troops would leave Korea soon after.

Truman accepted MacArthur's assessment. He wanted
MacArthur to be right because he hoped to gain political support
as a result of a successful conclusion to the Korean conflict.

Besides, MacArthur's opinions on the Chinese situation were
shared by some of Truman's own advisers. As recently as
September 13, 1950, Dean Acheson had expressed similar views
on the subject of communist China:

A North Korean tank and bridge south of Suwon lie in ruin after an attack by UN forces.

I should think it would be sheer madness on the part of the Chinese Communists to [interfere]. Now, I give the people in Beijing credit for being intelligent enough to see what is happening to them. Why they would want to further their own dismemberment and destruction by getting at cross purposes with all the free nations of the world who are inherently their friends and have always been the friends of the Chinese against this imperialism coming down from the Soviet Union I cannot see.

The Joint Chiefs of Staff seemed to be in agreement. Indeed, Gen. Omar Bradley, chairman of the Joint Chiefs of Staff, told the president that "no unilateral move by Red China" could be expected because the country "lacked the military power." Clearly, Bradley discounted the possibility of a Chinese attack.

So UN troops, under the overall direction of MacArthur in Tokyo, prepared to march north. MacArthur flew to Korea to see the campaign get started. He gathered together his corps commanders for an encouraging send-off. "Gentlemen," MacArthur told his officers,

The war is over. The Chinese are not coming into this war. In less than two weeks the Eighth Army will close on the Yalu across the entire front. The 3rd Division will be back at Fort Benning for Christmas dinner.

An aerial view (left) shows bombs exploding near the Yalu River. After the attack, UN troops (right) await further orders.

Military communications were difficult to maintain in the hills of Korea.

The UN Divisions

MacArthur divided the UN forces under his command into two groups. One group included the Eighth Army under the command of Lt. Gen. Walton H. Walker and X Corps commanded by Maj. Gen. Edward M. Almond. They were directed to head north toward the Chinese border.

The first prize of the campaign was Pyongyang, the capital of North Korea. A race developed between the American and South Korean units for the honor of capturing the city. When the South Koreans reached Pyongyang on October 20, however, the event was anticlimactic. Most of the North Korean soldiers and Soviets in the Soviet embassy had already fled the rubble-strewn city. One soldier reported that the "single prize was a warehouse chock-full of canned food and whiskey, which the hungry GIs greedily devoured."

MacArthur was delighted with the success of his forces and urged them to move at full speed toward the Yalu River, the dividing line between North Korea and the Chinese province of Manchuria. In defiance of specific instructions to the contrary, MacArthur ordered both American and ROK forces to move toward the Chinese border.

The Eighth Army under General Walker proceeded up the west coast of the Korean peninsula. X Corps, largely marines and some ROK divisions, under General Almond headed north along the narrow, steep, mountainous trails on the east side of the peninsula. These troops were to arrive at the border from two directions.

By proceeding in this manner, General MacArthur violated some of the most basic rules of military science. He divided his small force and sent them against the potential might of the Chinese troops, who were close to their own base of supplies. Moreover, the Eighth Army and X Corps could not communicate by phone because of the height of the hills separating them. They could not assist one another in case of attack because they were separated by a twenty-to-thirty-mile gap.

MacArthur began to receive reports from his field commanders that they had seen Chinese soldiers among the North Korean troops. But MacArthur urged the UN forces on until one American unit from the Eighth Army actually reached the Yalu River late in October 1950.

On returning from the Yalu, that unit was surrounded by Chinese forces and largely destroyed in a savage attack. The Chinese then engaged other units in an action that lasted four days. Then, in one of the strangest events of military history, the victorious Chinese communist forces left the field of battle on November 6. French troops reported seeing them withdraw into the hills. They had disappeared. Acheson told President Truman in Washington that "they seemed to have vanished from the face of the earth."

From Tokyo, MacArthur took this departure to mean that only a few Chinese soldiers stood between the UN forces and the Yalu River and complete victory. He did not see it as a warning of the potential strength of the enemy. Nor did he remember his instructions to withdraw rather than engage Chinese troops.

Boldly, MacArthur announced the beginning of what he and most people believed would be the final campaign of the Korean War. On November 24, MacArthur launched his "home by Christmas" campaign.

CHAPTER THREE

Communist China Enters the Conflict

In the winter of 1950, Chinese communist soldiers entered North Korea to help their communist allies. These Chinese soldiers completely changed the nature of the Korean War. The United Nations now faced a formidable enemy with huge manpower resources. The Chinese could also draw on nearby resources of food, ammunition, and winter clothing. In the following months, the UN forces would face difficulties that were much greater than what they had anticipated in June 1950.

The Chinese entry into the war came soon after the North Korean retreat from the south. MacArthur's successful landing at Inchon in September had forced the North Koreans to lift their siege of Pusan in the southeast corner of South Korea. They hurriedly retreated north in a desperate effort to escape from South Korea.

The Chinese communist leaders, Mao Tse-tung and Chou En-lai, knew that the remnants of this North Korean army had ceased to be a major factor either on the battlefield or in the political field. The NKPA was greatly reduced in numbers and had left much of its equipment behind during its flight north. The NKPA no longer could serve as a buffer to defend the Chinese border against invaders.

In this changing situation, the Chinese communists received military and political support from the Soviet Union. This support enabled them to deploy hundreds of thousands of troops both in Manchuria and in hidden advance positions across the Yalu River in North Korea. If the UN advance continued, the Chinese intended to strike.

The Chinese anxiously followed the progress of the UN armies as they advanced toward the Manchurian border in late October and early November. Chinese leaders decided that the objective of the UN forces had changed. Instead of the original goal of recapturing and restoring an independent South Korea, Chinese leaders believed that the United Nations intended to attack communist China and overthrow its government.

China Questions U.S. Objectives

The Chinese warning to the United Nations on October 3 had been ignored. The Communist party of China issued an additional warning on November 4:

> The situation today is very clear. The United States imperialists are copying the old trick of the Japanese bandits—first invading Korea and then invading China. Everyone knows that Korea is a small country, but that its strategic position is very important. Just as the Japanese imperialists in the past, the main objective of the United States aggression in Korea is not Korea itself but China.

The Chinese statement was a public announcement of their fear of attack. They warned the United Nations, and particularly the United States, that they intended to defend their borders. There were important hydroelectric facilities along the Yalu River, and the Chinese intended to protect this vital source of power.

By November, there were perhaps as many as half a million Chinese troops just north of the border. Meanwhile, the UN armies continued to move northward. They fought the retreating North Koreans, they fought the steep and treacherous mountains of North Korea, and they prepared to fight the encroaching winter.

As they advanced toward the Chosin Reservoir, General Walker of the Eighth Army and General Almond in command of X Corps grew increasingly uneasy. Many units were already tired and had suffered serious casualties in the northern advance. General MacArthur, however, dismissed their concerns and urged them forward.

The UN troops, numbering 150,000 men trudged onward, hoping the war would soon be over. Unfortunately, they soon encountered "human waves" of Chinese troops who fought with the ferocity of people defending their homes. The hope of a quick end to the war soon disappeared.

On November 8, 1950, several air battles took place between American and Soviet-built planes near the North Korean-Chinese border. The American planes were largely driven by propellers. They were efficient, and the pilots flew them well, but they were clearly no match against the Soviet MIG-15 jet fighters they

American F-86 jets were deployed to reduce the North Korean air threat.

encountered. This was the first jet battle in history, and the American planes were outclassed. The air battle was an additional warning that the Chinese border would be defended fiercely and that the communist planes could easily shoot the slower American planes out of the sky.

Chinese Soldiers Shock Walker

General Walker was unaware of the exact size of the enemy forces he faced. But the several Chinese soldiers his scouts captured came as a shock to Walker. He expected, as MacArthur had told him, that the Chinese would not enter the fight. Because the prisoners came from several different Chinese divisions, Walker began to suspect that the size of the opposing armies was formidable.

UN troops were unprepared for the cold Korean winter.

The worsening weather added to the discomfort of Walker and his multinational forces. The first snows of the winter began to fall, and the temperatures dropped dramatically. The UN troops had not prepared for a winter campaign, and in the inhospitable Korean climate, winter weather could defeat soldiers as effectively as an enemy army.

Walker assessed the position of his troops and began to consider a halt to the campaign. Stocks of food and ammunition were low. Winter clothing was in desperately short supply. It would be extremely difficult to carry supplies over the winter roads to the widely scattered UN forces. Communication among the units was difficult to maintain. The situation appeared to be grim indeed.

A *New York Times* reporter traveling with the Eighth Army described the condition of the UN troops on November 15:

The men have been cold night and day and it appears that additional snow is arriving. The men of the First Cavalry have received most of their winter clothes but they still lack their heavy field overcoats and critically needed heavy "shoepacks," the Army's new Arctic boots and heavy socks to go with them. The doctors have started treating the first cases of trenchfoot, an affliction that was to have been made a thing of the past by the "shoepacks."

General Walker reported these conditions to General Mac-Arthur. He complained that the troops were poorly equipped and suffered greatly from the extremely cold November temperatures:

No one had insulated footwear and many had no gloves, while the clothing supply generally was short of winter gear. Food supplies were just barely sufficient. At one point along the march a four-man patrol volunteered to search out a crossing place for their battalion in a swift-running stream. Despite the merciless cold, the men waded into the nearly waist-deep river, and they were almost immediately encased in ice. They had to be put promptly into a warming tent and have their clothing cut off.

MacArthur, however, did not worry about these conditions. He continued to assure his field commanders that the Chinese would not intervene in Korea. MacArthur and his intelligence staff ignored the ominous information obtained from both the field commanders and the Chinese prisoners.

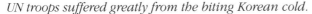

UN troops suffered greatly from the biting Korean cold.

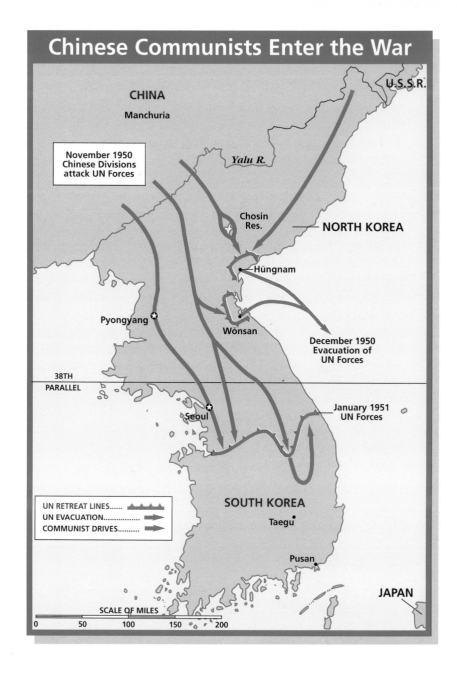

Chinese Communists Enter the War

CHINA

Manchuria

U.S.S.R.

November 1950
Chinese Divisions
attack UN Forces

Yalu R.

Chosin Res.

NORTH KOREA

Hŭngnam

Pyongyang

Wŏnsan

December 1950
Evacuation of
UN Forces

38TH
PARALLEL

January 1951
UN Forces

Seoul

SOUTH KOREA

Taegu

UN RETREAT LINES......
UN EVACUATION.................
COMMUNIST DRIVES..........

Pusan

JAPAN

SCALE OF MILES

0   50   100   150   200

It's Almost Over

From Tokyo, MacArthur continued to assure his men and the Truman administration that the war was almost over. No one dared openly question MacArthur's judgment. Gen. Matthew Ridgway explained that "a more subtle result of the Inchon triumph was the development of an almost superstitious regard for General MacArthur's infallibility and even his superiors, it seemed, began to doubt if they should question any of MacArthur's decisions." To say that the Chinese were in Korea, historian Robert Smith explains, would be to suggest "that MacArthur was wrong. And there were very few who dared."

The Chinese communist troops, however, continued to build up their forces, make their plans, and wait. On November 24, MacArthur gave the order for a "general offensive" toward the Yalu River. This order was given not only to the ROK troops but also to both the Eighth Army and those in X Corps to the east. These American troops had been expressly forbidden by President Truman from advancing on the Chinese border.

The Chinese Attack

On November 25, the Chinese struck. Eighteen fresh Chinese divisions with many soldiers in warm, quilted, heavy winter uniforms attacked the overextended lines of the Eighth Army on the west coast of North Korea.

The Chinese attacked the strung out advance units of the Eighth Army both from the front and from the side. Because X Corps and the Eighth Army were widely separated, X Corps could not come to Walker's assistance. Each force had to face its agony alone.

In the initial Chinese attacks against the Eighth Army, the communists almost completely destroyed the South Korean divisions Walker had placed on his right flank. Terrified of the Chinese, the South Koreans who were not killed or captured ran from the Chinese in complete disorder.

This development endangered the entire Eighth Army. The Chinese communists threatened to envelop the right wing of the army, attack it in small pieces, and destroy the UN forces. The Eighth

Snow and ice added to the hardship of the Korean conflict.

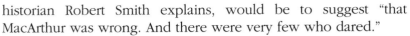

Chinese Tactics

Chinese armies relied less upon finesse than upon mass strength and sustaining and inflicting huge losses in order to win battles. The Chinese army simply did not display the same concern for the preservation of life that tended to characterize the UN forces.

They had primitive equipment. They had few modern methods of communication—telephones were reserved for the most senior officers. Therefore, in order to communicate instructions, various units resorted to other means of communication. Bugle blowing, sudden explosions of firepower, and shrill whistle blasts were used to signal the onset of battle, for example. Since the Chinese tried to attack small units from all directions simultaneously, the tremendous noise that signaled the beginning of an action would terrify and confuse the UN forces.

This confusion obscured the fact that many communist soldiers were unarmed. Most Chinese soldiers had only hand grenades. Frequently, only one soldier in five went into battle with a gun. The Chinese soldiers were supposed to pick up the weapons of fallen comrades. But often, these were only spears fashioned from pieces of automobile springs attached to poles.

Chinese Warning

On the night of October 2, 1950, Kavalam Madhava Panikkar, the Indian ambassador to China, was summoned from his bed by Chinese foreign minister Chou En-lai and asked to send a message to the West. That message, delivered on October 3, announced that if American troops crossed the 38th parallel, they would "encounter Chinese resistance."

The Chinese government decided to deliver the message through the Indian ambassador for two reasons. The Indian delegation was believed to be aligned neither with the Soviet Union nor the United States. Also, because a close friendship existed between India and China, at that time, the warning would be accepted as reliable.

The Chinese warning was ignored by President Truman and his advisers. They considered Ambassador Panikkar to be sympathetic to the communist side. In addition, the message from Chou En-lai was delivered after Truman had decided to cross the 38th parallel. The administration in Washington did not want to appear to be afraid of the Chinese by changing its military plans in the face of a third-party warning.

Korean refugees flee south with UN troops.

Army was stunned and astonished by the endless number of Chinese troops descending upon it. A halt was called to the advance but the halt turned into confusion. Soon, in terror, most units of the Eighth Army boarded whatever vehicles still moved in the snow and subzero temperatures—weapons carriers, trucks, tractors, and tanks—and fled in the face of the Chinese communist armies.

Eighth Army headquarters, far in the rear of the UN forces at Taegu, did not immediately understand the extent of the military retreat. Therefore, military leaders failed to rally the fleeing troops at strategic points. Even the massive air support from the Fifth Air Force, which took an appalling toll on the Chinese units, did not stop the retreat.

The retreat eventually extended along a 130-mile route, from the Chongchon River near the North Korean border to the Imjin River north of Seoul. It became the longest retreat in all of American military history.

Bug Out

The motorized Eighth Army units "bugged out," or left so quickly that most of the soldiers soon lost contact with the enemy. More slowly, the Chinese forces relentlessly continued moving south after them. The Chinese soldiers traveled by foot and moved easily over the snow-covered mountains and icebound rivers of Korea. They moved easily because they traveled lightly, without transport, and usually with about a six-day supply of rice on their backs.

The vehicles of the UN forces, however, were forced to travel on the treacherous mountain roads of Korea. There were frequent breakdowns. Often, trucks stopped in the middle of the road, creating roadblocks for the troops behind as well as for the thousands of Korean refugees who followed in their wake.

These innocent victims of the war attempted to get out of the path of the advancing Chinese armies, which were assisted by smaller North Korean units. The refugees knew how viciously the communists treated their prisoners. The refugees feared losing their homes, their property, and their lives. A soldier who participated in the retreat described one scene: "There were literally millions of refugees blocking the road by sheer mass, the silent columns moving without hope, shelter or food, avoiding others' tragedies of death, loss of total possessions, and those who simply sank to the ground too tired and defeated to move, the tossing away of babies, borne on their mothers' backs and now frozen to death."

Gene Symonds of the United Press found himself in the midst of these refugees and called the Korean conflict "the ugly war." He shared with his readers the scenes of human tragedy he encountered on the flight from the Yalu River:

> The handsome young Korean woman lay sprawled beside the road. One breast was bared to the winter wind, and her arms were frozen in the position she held her baby. Next to her in the snowbank was the baby, swaddled in rags, its frozen face peering out.
>
> The mother and child were only two of the many refugees killed along the road. Bodies of refugees had been dragged to the side of the road. Some spots where the snow and frozen blood had melted were turned brown. Blankets and children's clothes, bits of clothing and small tots' articles were strewn along the road in confusion. At one place I saw a tiny red baby cap with something in it in the mud. I did not see the baby.

Such scenes were repeated in hundreds of places as refugees sought safety from the advancing enemy that showed no sympathy for the frightened, hungry, and confused civilian victims of the war.

X Corps Advance Also Disastrous

While the refugees and dispirited Eighth Army sought refuge in the south, another drama—more heroic but equally disastrous—was taking place in the northeast. There, X Corps also tried to reach the Yalu River but soon faced total destruction.

American marines and American and British army units advanced through the deep snows and frigid temperatures of the mountains of North Korea. They advanced toward the border in three widely separated columns. They worked their way north around the Chosin and Fusan reservoirs, which are about

Yalu River

During the November 1950 offensive, reaching the Yalu River became a major objective for the UN forces. The UN forces wanted to bomb the many bridges across the river that allowed the Chinese armies to cross to the south. They also wanted to hit the hydroelectric plants located near the river.

United Nations strategic planners understood that crossing the river would cause China to enter the war. American pilots were given specific instructions never to cross Chinese airspace north of the Yalu River in pursuit of Chinese planes. Nor were American pilots permitted to bomb the northern ends of the many bridges spanning the Yalu River. The UN forces knew that large numbers of Chinese or Soviet air units might enter into the conflict. UN bomber pilots and General MacArthur complained about the military unfairness of permitting the Chinese MIGs to escape into Manchuria. On the other hand, the Chinese pilots also seemed to have recognized and accepted UN air supremacy over Korea and did not venture much south of the Yalu River in their efforts to protect Chinese airspace. As a result, the Yalu River served both as a geographic and psychological barrier between the opposing forces during the conflict.

thirty-four hundred feet above sea level. Some small units actually reached the Yalu River.

On November 26, twelve Chinese divisions attacked General Almond and his forces. The first fury of the Chinese thrust fell upon several isolated marine regiments. The marines held out heroically, often engaging in hand-to-hand fighting. Many UN units were completely destroyed. Tragically, 1,450 of the original 2,500 marines of these advance regiments died in this attack. By the end of the campaign, only 380 had survived unharmed.

The entire X Corps soon faced annihilation at the hands of well-disciplined and superior Chinese forces. At one point, X Corps units fought the enemy almost nonstop night and day for seventy-two hours. Much of this fighting was hand-to-hand combat.

During this ordeal, the marines learned never to zip up their sleeping bags. At night, the Chinese would elude the guards, slip into fortified camps, and bayonet men as they struggled to free themselves to grab their weapons.

On December 1, the marines decided to try to fight their way out of North Korea rather than stay and be destroyed. They buried the bodies of their fallen comrades in holes they blew in the frozen ground. Then, taking along their wounded, most of their equipment, and even some Chinese prisoners, more than ten thousand troops began the dangerous retreat to the coast that General Almond ironically called "an attack to the rear."

Retreat

Following procedures, the marines executed an orderly fighting withdrawal, assisted throughout by navy planes, which acted as a shield against some of the Chinese advances. The Chinese stationed themselves on the hills overlooking the narrow road leading to safety. The navy planes raked the hill emplacements with bombs, frequently dropping napalm, a thick and sticky substance that burns the skin, on the Chinese who tried to ambush the retreating UN forces.

The long, winding columns of marines made their slow way back down the sides of the Chosin Reservoir along tiny, dangerous trails. Frequently, especially at night when their airplanes could not assist them, the marines were attacked by the Chinese. The marines had to work their way around Chinese-built roadblocks. They built makeshift mountain bridges to carry away their wounded and their vehicles.

The marines and other UN forces made their way back from the towns of Yudam and Hudong and gathered at Hagaru at the base of the Chosin Reservoir. There, they joined forces with the several thousand defenders of Hagaru and found the supplies they had wisely stored away on their way toward the Yalu River early in November.

At Hagaru, still sixty-four mountain miles from the relative safety of the port of Hungnam, there was a tiny airstrip. The marines had begun the construction of that strip on November 19 as a precautionary measure. Through great effort, they had hauled five large bulldozers through the mountains to Hagaru, where they hacked out the strip from the frozen ground. By December 1, the marines had managed to clear a strip in the mountains twenty-nine hundred feet long and fifty feet wide.

Given the jagged terrain and frozen ground, the construction of even this tiny strip was something of a miracle. But would it be long enough for planes to land and rescue the wounded?

The official manuals called for a minimum of seventy-six hundred feet of landing room for the C-47 transport planes that would fly into the Korean mountains. Nevertheless, C-47s landed on the airstrip without a single mishap and airlifted 4,312 wounded men to safety in five days without losing a single plane.

Once the wounded men were rescued, the marines continued their slow, orderly withdrawal from Hagaru to the sea and safety. All along the way, they were attacked by Chinese forces that set up roadblocks and fired down from the hills on the retreating UN forces. But the navy planes kept up their daytime protection of the marines. During the final withdrawal, the planes appeared to swarm over the UN forces like a huge umbrella.

As the marines fought their way south, the U.S. Navy made preparations to withdraw the survivors of the long, frigid trek from the North Korean mountains. Aircraft carriers moved into position off the coast of Hungnam. Planes from the carriers attacked enemy positions behind the lines of the escaping X Corps survivors. Along with the land-based Corsairs, the planes from the aircraft carriers flew endless missions against the

American fighter pilots flew hundreds of missions against Chinese forces, protecting UN ground troops.

F-40 Corsairs return from a North Korean combat mission. Below them is the USS Boxer.

A ground crew (left) readies a fighter plane for another mission. A wounded soldier (right) awaits medical attention.

Chinese, and the last, tired, battered remnants of X Corps finally arrived at Hungnam on December 11, 1950.

Losses during this heroic retreat had been heavy. The United Nations had lost more than 2,000 men before the retreat had begun on December 1. The breakout itself resulted in 718 additional battle deaths and many other nonfatal casualties, many of them from frostbite.

The cost to the Chinese was much higher. It was estimated that the Chinese suffered more than forty thousand casualties as they followed X Corps south toward Hungnam.

Between December 11 and December 24, 1950, dockers at Hungnam loaded 105,000 American, British, and Korean military personnel, more than 90,000 Korean refugees, 350,000 tons of cargo, and more than 17,500 vehicles that would be used later. The UN forces destroyed whatever remained on shore as the last ship departed from Hungnam.

The Hungnam evacuation was one of the most sensational escapes recorded during the Korean War. Within a few days, X Corps landed at Pusan, where the survivors were treated for their many medical problems and regained their strength.

But wars are not won by achieving great escapes. The Chinese communists had caused serious damage to the UN forces, had shattered their optimism, and had cast doubt on the goals of the entire conflict.

The UN command had to reexamine its objectives and develop a new strategy. The first step was to place X Corps and the Eighth Army under a unified command. The next step would be a change in leadership. Matthew B. Ridgway would soon assume complete direction of the UN forces in Korea.

CHAPTER FOUR

War on the Home Front

During the Korean War, the United States became the most powerful and richest industrial and military nation on earth. World War II had not touched American shores or destroyed American farms, cities, and transportation systems, as it had in Europe. As a result, the country experienced enormous growth both during and after the war. Workers, farmers, and businesspeople shared the fruits of this victory. The country did not have to endure the daily deprivations that accompany most long wars.

But all was not well at home. During the years of the Korean conflict, the United States experienced one of the darkest, most repressive periods in all of its history. These years were marred by the great communist or "red" scare in the United States.

Because of the red scare, Truman had to contend with two separate struggles. Abroad, he fought to keep the South Korean government from falling to the North Korean communists. At home, he fought political opponents who used lies, intimidation, and scare tactics to tie the president to a "communist conspiracy" and thereby to control his conduct of foreign policy. These same opponents tried to destroy the careers of those men closest to Truman in order to reduce the power of the presidency and increase the power of Congress.

The Democrat

Republicans accused Truman of being responsible for Soviet gains all over the world. They charged that "deals" had been

House Un-American Activities Committee

The House Un-American Activities Committee (HUAC) was established in 1945 as the first standing, or permanent, committee in the House of Representatives. It grew out of a similar committee first formed on a temporary basis in 1938 and headed by a conservative Texas Democrat, Martin Dies. The Dies Committee and later the HUAC had the same objectives. They were formed to fight a perceived threat "to the American way of life" from the American Communist party and its sympathizers.

Conservative Republicans and southern Democrats formed the coalition that supported the HUAC. The chairmen of the HUAC and many of its members believed that not only communists but also New Deal Democrats, socialists, labor union members, blacks, Jews, intellectuals, and liberals were dangerous and should be watched. The committee used large amounts of government money to unearth perceived plots to aid the Soviet Union.

The committee used highly irregular techniques during its hearings to expose "traitors." The HUAC ignored sound rules of evidence, ruined the reputations of political opponents, and used the press to increase the atmosphere of fear in the United States.

The committee began to keep a file on all those Americans it considered dangerous. At one point, the committee's list consisted of more than one million names, stored in six hundred file cabinets. The list was consulted to verify the "loyalty" of people being considered for employment. Even the name of child movie star Shirley Temple appeared on the committee's list of Americans of questionable loyalty.

Two members of the HUAC introduced legislation, called the Mundt Bill, that required the registration of members of the Communist party and all organizations associated with it. Failure to register would result in prosecution; registration left an individual open to arrest. The Mundt Bill effectively outlawed the Communist party in the United States. The fear of communism was so great that the bill passed the House by a vote of 319 to 58.

One of the most active members of the HUAC and a cosponsor of the Mundt Bill was a young congressman from California named Richard M. Nixon. Nixon opposed what he considered the "coddling," or pampering, of communists by the Truman administration. He believed that treason by American agents led to the fall of China and eventually to the Korean War.

Skillfully, Nixon used his membership on the HUAC to advance his own career. In fact, Nixon decided to stake his political future on linking Alger Hiss, a friend of Secretary of State Dean Acheson, to the Communist party.

Hiss appeared before the HUAC to refute charges that he had been a spy for the Communist party in the 1930s. Nixon pursued Hiss relentlessly, even when most of the committee was prepared to accept his protests of innocence. A nine-hour public hearing conducted by the HUAC regarding Hiss's testimony enabled Nixon to gain national attention as one of the most effective members of the committee.

The committee also published a series of booklets that were intended to assist ordinary citizens in identifying communists in all walks of life.

During its long and turbulent career in the 1940s and 1950s, the HUAC became an instrument for attacking American traditions of fairness, equality before the law, freedom of speech, and other constitutional guarantees. Committee members employed tactics that intimidated those who appeared before it. Americans who condemned HUAC activities were denounced as communist sympathizers. Many opponents soon fell silent out of fear. Such people may have agreed with the sentiments expressed by Harry Truman, who said the HUAC was "more un-American than the activities it is investigating."

made by communists close to Roosevelt and Truman that resulted in the "giveaway" of eastern and central Europe to the Soviets. Republicans hinted broadly that many of those responsible for these losses were still working in the State Department.

The Republicans suggested that Truman's reluctance to commit forces to the Far East was a result of the influence exercised by communist sympathizers in the State Department. Such people were supposedly more interested in increasing the strength of international communism than in forwarding the interests of the United States.

Tracking Down the Communists

Republicans, aided by conservative southern Democrats, launched a major campaign to hunt out communists and to link them to Truman.

This communist hunt was tolerated by the American public. Communists in the United States had long been objects of popular fear and targets of the government. The Communist party's freedom had been severely curtailed since the end of World War II. In 1950, over Truman's veto, Congress passed the McCarran Internal Security Act.

The McCarran Act made it unlawful "to combine, conspire, or agree with any other person to perform any act which would substantially contribute to…the establishment of a totalitarian dictatorship." The act required American communists to register with the attorney general of the United States as foreign agents. It also kept immigrants with communist backgrounds from entering the country. Enforcement of the McCarran Act was placed under the jurisdiction of the newly established Subversive Activities Control Board.

Truman denounced the act, saying it "put the Government into the business of thought control." The president believed that the McCarran Act would endanger freedom of speech and freedom of assembly.

In turn, Republicans charged that the president and Secretary of State Dean Acheson were "soft on Communism," and perhaps not fit for office. Republicans exploited Truman's veto of the act as a sign of support for dangerous elements in the government.

The increasingly bitter exchanges between Truman and Republican members of Congress formed the backdrop for a hunt for communists both inside and outside of government. Many Americans were afraid to speak out against the government or hold meetings that could be interpreted as opposing the government for fear that they would be labeled communists. One cynic noted that the chief justice of the Supreme Court said that "if the Bill of Rights were put to a vote, it would lose."

Making Lists

Republicans combed the pages of communist newspapers to compile lists of names of suspected communists. They worked through the voluminous files of the House Un-American Activities Committee, searching for the names of prominent individuals to investigate.

Their campaign gained popularity and support when Republicans uncovered federal employees with communist backgrounds, such as Judith Coplon, a former employee of the Justice Department; Klaus Fuchs, who had turned over important American atomic secrets to the Soviet Union; and Julius and Ethel Rosenberg, who were tried and executed on charges of treason. The Republicans also gained the cooperation of known communists such as Whittaker Chambers, a senior editor of *Time* magazine.

Chambers's testimony before the House Un-American Activities Committee provided Republicans with their most damning "evidence" against the Truman administration. Chambers charged that Alger Hiss, a person with strong links to the Truman administration, had been involved in spying for the Soviet Union during the 1930s.

Alger Hiss had been an important member of Franklin Roosevelt's administration and had served the government during the war years. Hiss had strongly supported the New Deal legislation of the 1930s. Because of that support, he personally symbolized for many Americans the social advances made during the Roosevelt era. And so he was the perfect target for the anti-New Deal, anti-Truman Republicans.

In response to Whittaker Chambers's accusations, Hiss was called before the House Un-American Activities Committee to answer charges that he had spied for the Soviet Union. President

Ethel and Julius Rosenberg (left and far right) were tried for passing secret atomic information to the Soviets. They were convicted and executed.

Alger Hiss

Alger Hiss, born in 1904, graduated Phi Beta Kappa from Johns Hopkins University in 1926 and from Harvard Law School in 1929. After graduation, he served as a law clerk for the distinguished Supreme Court justice Oliver Wendell Holmes. When Franklin Delano Roosevelt took office in 1933, Hiss entered the Democratic administration and served with distinction in the Departments of Agriculture, Justice, and State.

Hiss was closely associated with Roosevelt's New Deal legislation, which completely changed the course of American social and governmental history. In a dramatic break with past Republican administrations, the central government grew tremendously and assumed many new responsibilities. It actively played a role in reducing the hardships of daily life through the passage of a mass of social legislation.

Hiss was also associated with Roosevelt's foreign policies. He went with the president to Yalta in 1945 as a political adviser. In San Francisco later that year, Hiss was elected temporary secretary general of the United Nations conference.

In 1947, Hiss resigned from his position in the State Department. He took up the task of heading the prestigious Carnegie Endowment for International Peace.

In 1948, an editor at *Time* magazine named Whittaker Chambers told the House Un-American Activities Committee that Hiss was a former Soviet spy. Chambers accused Hiss of having stolen important documents from the government in the 1930s with the intent of revealing their secrets to the Soviets.

Whittaker Chambers went to his Maryland farm where he located copies of these documents that he had concealed in some pumpkins. The "pumpkin papers" gained great notoriety and added to the growing fear of communism in the country.

Hiss sued Chambers for slander, which is accusing someone of false charges. The first Hiss trial ended in a hung jury. But the second trial, held in 1950, found Hiss to be guilty of perjury. He could not be convicted on any possible treason charges because the statute of limitations had expired. Hiss was sentenced to a five-year prison term. In 1954, Hiss was released from prison after having served three years of his term. He returned to private life and continued to assert his innocence.

Alger Hiss was accused of intending to reveal government secrets to the Soviets.

Sen. Joseph R. McCarthy believed communists had infiltrated the highest levels of U.S. government.

Truman defended Hiss and called the investigation against him a "red herring." Nevertheless, under very close and persistent questioning, Hiss revealed that he had associated with Chambers during the 1930s. Eventually, Hiss was tried and convicted of perjury, or lying before the committee, and was sent to prison.

The Hiss trial added fuel to the anti-Truman Republican campaign. Republicans publicly announced connections between communists such as Hiss in the State Department and the communist takeover of China. In the growing anticommunist hysteria of the period, few people dared challenge the connection. The atmosphere of distrust and intimidation allowed political opportunists to use the fear of communism to quiet their opposition.

McCarthy and the Red Scare

In particular, the red scare attracted the attention of a Wisconsin senator named Joseph R. McCarthy. McCarthy was a first-term senator in danger of losing the next election. He needed an issue to help him gain the attention of the voters in his state.

McCarthy decided that the red scare could be the key to his political success. The dark-bearded, heavy-drinking McCarthy spoke to audiences throughout the country on the dangers of communism in government. The following excerpt from a February 9, 1950 speech, is typical of the techniques he used to fuel the fear of communism: "While I cannot take the time to name all the men in the State Department who have been named as members of the Communist party...I have here in my hand a list of two hundred and five that were known to the Secretary of State as being members of the Communist party and who, nevertheless, are still working and shaping policy in the State Department."

Joseph McCarthy

Joseph Raymond McCarthy (1908–1957), a Wisconsin attorney, circuit court judge, and World War II marine, gained his greatest fame as a Republican senator. In 1946, he was elected to Congress as a result of a startling victory over the popular Wisconsin senator Robert M. La Follette. But between 1946 and 1950, McCarthy had an undistinguished career in Washington, D.C. He needed an issue that would keep his name in the news and ensure his reelection to the Senate in 1952.

McCarthy's attention was drawn to the rising tide of isolationism, anticommunism, and antiforeign sentiment in the country. He decided to further his own political career by exploiting these fears.

McCarthy effectively used the "big lie" technique, which was especially powerful when presented through the new medium of television, to accuse political opponents. He accused many prominent members of the government, and especially those people closest to President Truman, of having ties with the Communist party. When these people tried to refute these outrageous claims, McCarthy simply moved on to another charge. The accusations were never proved.

On February 9, 1950, in Wheeling, West Virginia, McCarthy first used the techniques that would gain him fame and notoriety. At a major political gathering, he announced that the American government was filled with communists and communist sympathizers. He held up a sheet of paper that he said contained a list of the names of many communists who actively were subverting the government.

McCarthy hedged when pressed to "reveal" the names of those people. In the end, he never uncovered a single communist agent in the U.S. government. But that did not stop McCarthy from continuing his attack on the government and particularly on Secretary of State Dean Acheson.

The Wisconsin senator strongly opposed Acheson's foreign policy, arguing that it had led to the fall of China to communism. McCarthy accused Acheson of harboring more than two hundred "known communists" within the State Department. Supposedly, these people were involved in working for the Soviets and in undermining the interests of the United States. McCarthy linked these "agents" with a "spy ring" that had assisted the communist cause in the Far East.

Fueled by McCarthy's irresponsible behavior, a kind of mass hysteria seized the country. Before McCarthy was finally revealed to be a vindictive, self-serving fraud, thousands of Americans lost their reputations and their jobs as a wild hunt for communists took place.

Unfortunately, the temporary hysteria played an important role in the development of American foreign policy in the 1950s. It forced Truman to take a stronger position against the North Koreans and the Chinese communists than he might otherwise have adopted. It also forced him to ignore the shortcomings of Syngman Rhee and Chiang Kai-shek, who were seen as anticommunist heroes in the eyes of McCarthyites. To act otherwise might lead to charges of being "soft on communism." In the atmosphere of the 1950s, such a charge could erode public trust and political support for the president at home and threaten the war effort.

In the end, Joseph McCarthy was labeled as an "irresponsible, self-seeking witch-hunter who was undermining the nation's tradition of civil liberties." In 1952, as chairman of the Government Committee on Operations of the Senate, McCarthy hurled wild, unsubstantiated charges against many noted Americans. In 1954, television cameras provided the nation with the spectacle of thirty-six hours of congressional hearings in which the senator's brutal treatment of witnesses lost him much public support.

In that same year, the Senate, now dominated by Democrats, voted to condemn McCarthy for conduct "contrary to Senate traditions."

Douglas MacArthur

Douglas MacArthur (1880–1964) was a great American general and commander in chief of the Allied forces in the southwest Pacific Ocean during World War II. He graduated first in his class from West Point and was an aloof and commanding figure whose personal style led one journalist to call him the "Caesar of the Pacific."

MacArthur was in command of American forces on the Philippine Islands during the Japanese attack on Pearl Harbor. He received radio information that the attack had taken place and that the Japanese were attacking American military, naval, and air installations. However, he failed to act to protect his own ships and planes, and like those at Pearl Harbor, his were caught and destroyed on the ground, approximately nine hours after the sneak attack on Pearl Harbor.

The American high command, however, did not take action against MacArthur. MacArthur was so popular with the American public that the military felt it would risk public support if they punished MacArthur. So, despite this and other costly mistakes MacArthur made in the Pacific, he continued to represent the hope for ultimate victory against the Japanese.

When the Philippine Islands fell to the Japanese, the American high command sent MacArthur to Australia. With the familiar corncob pipe in his mouth, MacArthur vowed that he would return. He did return to the Philippine Islands, with a squad of reporters to record the moment for a grateful nation and for posterity. For his efforts in the Allied cause, Douglas MacArthur emerged from World War II a five-star general, a field marshal, and virtual ruler of Japan.

He oversaw the occupation of Japan with a firm hand. He disarmed and demilitarized the country and saw to it that war criminals were tried and punished. He helped the country adopt a democratic constitution, although the Japanese were permitted to keep their emperor. MacArthur set the Japanese on the road to post-war prosperity.

But MacArthur was a poor choice as far as the U.S. relationship with the Soviet Union was concerned. MacArthur's anticommunist stance made the Soviets uncomfortable with the American occupation of Japan. The Soviet Union was concerned that the United States was building up an anti-Soviet state in Japan. In the words of MacArthur's biographer William Manchester, MacArthur was

> Flamboyant, imperious and apocalyptic, he carried the plumage of a flamingo, and could not acknowledge errors, and tried to cover up his mistakes with sly, childish tricks. Yet he was also endowed with great personal charm, a will of iron and a soaring intellect.

These were not the characteristics of a diplomat.

These characteristics, and MacArthur's view toward his political superiors in Washington that he, rather than they, should be making field decisions in wartime, played a major role in the way in which the Korean War was fought.

When the Korean War began, many officials doubted the wisdom of the decision to place MacArthur in control of the UN army. Dwight Eisenhower, who had served twice under MacArthur, was one of those who doubted the wisdom of giving MacArthur a free hand. Eisenhower told Gen. Matthew Ridgway that he would "like to see a younger general out there, rather than an untouchable whose actions you cannot predict, and who will himself decide what information he wants Washington to have and what he will withhold."

General MacArthur, reviewing American troops, thought President Truman was soft on communism.

McCarthy never uncovered any secret agent, never made any connection between Truman and a communist conspiracy, and never discovered an organized spy ring in the government. Nevertheless, he damaged many lives and helped to undermine the ability of the Truman administration to deal effectively with the Korean conflict.

MacArthur's Role in the Communist Hunt

Douglas MacArthur, commander of the UN forces in Korea, was supportive of McCarthy and the Republican party. MacArthur challenged Truman's conduct during the Korean War, saying Truman was soft on communism.

In 1951, Harry Truman faced the greatest crisis of his political career—he had to decide how to deal with Douglas MacArthur. The president was certain that if he did not do something about MacArthur soon, hundreds, perhaps thousands of additional American lives would be lost in a useless war against China. Truman also knew that if he did take action, his own political future was in jeopardy.

CHAPTER FIVE

Captain Fires General

This cartoonist claims that there were two sides to General MacArthur—that of soldier and politician.

Harry Truman became convinced that his disagreements with MacArthur meant that he must make a change in the military leadership. Truman had always disliked and distrusted Douglas MacArthur. He disapproved of the general's occasional failure to carry out his direct orders. In addition, Truman knew MacArthur often refused to explain his military plans to political superiors. The president particularly resented the general's public pronouncements to various press services that cast him in the most advantageous light. Truman believed that military officials should restrict their contacts with the press. Truman's view of MacArthur's arrogant behavior is reflected in the following verse written by an anonymous soldier:

> And while possibly a rumor now,
> Someday it will be fact
> That the Lord will hear a deep voice say
> Move over God—it's Mac.
>
> So bet your shoes that all the news
> That last great judgment day
> Will go to press in nothing less than
> Doug's Communique!

Truman's closest associates shared the president's opinion of the outspoken general. Dean Acheson called MacArthur a man of "incredible arrogance and vanity." Secretary of Defense George Marshall agreed with this assessment. President Truman, however, did not lose confidence in MacArthur because of his

Because he and MacArthur could no longer work together, Truman replaced him with Gen. Matthew Ridgway (far left).

administration's dislike of the general. After an agonizing nine months, Truman finally came to the decision that he and MacArthur could not work as a team in conducting the Korean War. The president decided to replace MacArthur with Matthew Ridgway. Ridgway was not a political general. Truman was certain that General Ridgway would carry out the limited military objectives that he had established.

The Truman-MacArthur controversy centered around the question of the proper relationship between the president of the United States and his military commander in the field. According to the Constitution, MacArthur was definitely stepping beyond his authority. The president is the commander in chief of the nation's armed forces. The president also directs American foreign policy. By violating Truman's orders, MacArthur was violating these principles.

Irreconcilable Differences

For nine months, Truman observed MacArthur's behavior and listened to his public statements. Truman concluded that MacArthur could not accept a subordinate role. The two men felt too differently about how the Korean conflict should be managed for them to continue in a working relationship.

Truman wanted to fight a limited war in Korea. MacArthur wanted to take the war beyond Korea into China in order to overthrow the communist government there. To fight that war,

Dean Acheson

Dean Acheson (1893–1971) was secretary of state under Harry Truman from 1949 to 1953. Educated at Yale and Harvard, he was an attorney with extensive experience in national affairs. He brought great knowledge and sophistication to Truman's administration. He was also known and trusted by the country's European allies.

Acheson's cultivated ways and somewhat chilly manner, however, alienated many people. But Harry Truman was very pleased that a man of such great learning and culture had become his friend and adviser.

Acheson was very much concerned with expanding American influence, not only in the Far East but also in Europe. In fact, he regarded the Soviet challenge to the United States to be greater in Europe than in Asia. Truman's Republican political enemies knew Acheson's opinions. As the war in Korea dragged on, Acheson became an easy target for those who disagreed with the Truman administration's refusal to fight an all-out war to unify the Korean peninsula. Many people blamed Acheson for guiding Truman away from commitment to a total war in Korea.

Final Offensives

SCALE OF MILES

0 50 100 150 200

UN DRIVES............................
UN RETREAT LINE........
COMMUNIST DRIVES..........
COMMUNIST RETREAT

U.S.S.R.

CHINA

Manchuria

Yalu R.

NORTH KOREA

Pyongyang

ARMISTICE LINE
(Truce signed
July 27, 1953)

38TH
PARALLEL

Panmunjom

Seoul

SOUTH KOREA

MacArthur urged the use of Chiang Kai-shek's Chinese Nationalist soldiers against mainland China. He also urged the blockading of Chinese harbors and suggested the use of atomic weapons in order to achieve victory.

MacArthur frequently offered these opinions to members of the press. He told them when he disagreed with Truman. When his own plans failed, he explained those failures as the consequence of lack of support on the part of the government.

This behavior is exemplified by the way in which MacArthur justified the outcome of his "home by Christmas" campaign. MacArthur had made many mistakes. He advanced to the Yalu River in November 1950 without preparing his troops for a winter campaign. He ignored reports of a huge enemy buildup. He recklessly sent Americans to the Manchurian border in defiance of presidential orders, and he divided his poorly fed and ill-clothed troops. These actions led a senior officer to observe that "MacArthur cared little for the common soldiers under his command nor the officers either."

But MacArthur did not accept responsibility for the failure of the campaign. Instead, he blamed the Truman administration for inadequate support. Specifically, MacArthur told various reporters that orders forbidding him to strike at communist targets in Manchuria put him under "an enormous handicap without precedent in military history." The major news services and the Tokyo papers gave the story wide coverage. The general had a huge following in the United States and was enormously popular.

No More Public Statements!

On December 5, 1950, Truman told MacArthur that he was to make no more public statements regarding administration policy. In the future, all public statements had to be cleared first by State Department or Defense Department officials. No private opinions were to be communicated to the press.

The general soon disregarded the order. In March 1951, Truman was secretly attempting to negotiate a settlement to end the Korean War. The Yalu campaign had convinced Truman that the United Nations should not try to unite Korea by military means. It should instead find a way to return to the division of the country along the 38th parallel. As a courtesy to his commander in the field, Truman told MacArthur about the confidential talks underway to achieve these objectives. MacArthur was warned not to discuss the negotiations publicly.

General MacArthur opposed Truman's peace plans. The general believed that "there was no substitute for victory." He publicly announced his opposition to the press. MacArthur

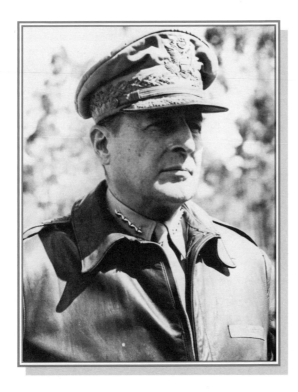

MacArthur thought that the Truman administration was supporting the war effort inadequately.

George Marshall

George Marshall (1880–1959), an outstanding general, had been a member of Gen. John Pershing's staff in World War I and was army chief of staff during World War II. In 1947, Marshall was called out of retirement to become secretary of state in Harry Truman's administration. He later replaced James V. Forrestal as secretary of defense.

As secretary of state, Marshall developed an economic recovery plan to assist in the reconstruction of devastated Western Europe after World War II and to help prevent that area from falling under communist control. That plan came to be known as the Marshall Plan. It was an enormous success, particularly since it allowed the countries involved to play the major role in determining how best to spend funds provided by the United States.

President Truman greatly valued Secretary of Defense Marshall's advice during the Korean War. The general shared a distrust of Douglas MacArthur, with whom he had worked during World War II. Marshall agreed with the president that the Korean conflict should have limited objectives.

Because of his strong support for the president, Marshall came under attack as being a communist sympathizer.

When Truman relieved MacArthur of his command, the general was forced to dismount from his proverbial high horse.

announced that if given control, he would recommend massive air strikes into China, the destruction of Chinese ports and shipping facilities, and even the "laying of radioactive waste cross the lines of enemy supply."

MacArthur claimed that he was unwilling to make a "sacrifice of the Korean nation." He demanded the unconditional surrender of the Chinese.

Truman issued an angry message to MacArthur directly ordering him not to make any more public statements. A *Washington Post* cartoon that appeared on March 31, 1951, graphically depicted the conflict between the general and the president. The cartoon showed Truman wagging a message under MacArthur's nose and saying, "Honest, no fooling this time!" In the cartoon, an undaunted general directs an aide to "file this one with the others."

But there was one more time. On April 5, 1951, the Republican minority leader of the House of Representatives, Joseph W. Martin, read before the full chamber a letter he had received from MacArthur. The general said that defeat of American forces in Asia would make the fall of Europe inevitable. "Victory would prevent war elsewhere," according to MacArthur. "As you point out," he wrote to Martin, "we must win. There is no substitute for victory."

This statement was the final straw. Truman at last decided to fire MacArthur. The president consulted with the Joint Chiefs of Staff as well as with his civilian advisers. They all agreed that MacArthur must go.

"I Want Him Fired"

Truman planned to send a delegation to Tokyo to inform MacArthur in person of his decision. Somehow, the news was leaked, and a rumor spread that MacArthur was about to retire. Truman was furious. He did not want to give MacArthur the opportunity to retire. Truman would not be denied the final word in the controversy with the general. So he quickly wired the orders to Tokyo on April 11, 1951, and the press was immediately informed of their contents. The president said, "The son of a bitch isn't going to resign on me. I want him fired."

The president expressed himself at greater length in his *Memoirs* as he explained why he fired Douglas MacArthur: "He prevented a cease-fire proposition.... I was ready to kick him into the North China Sea at that time. I was never so put out in all my life. It's the lowest trick a Commander-in-Chief can have done to him by an underling. MacArthur thought he was proconsul [the voice] for the government of the United States and could do as he damned pleased."

Gen. George Marshall, by 1950 the secretary of defense and a close associate of the president, agreed with this assessment of the situation. Marshall wrote: "What is new and what brought about the necessity for General MacArthur's removal is the entirely unprecedented situation of a local theatre commander publicly expressing his displeasure at and disagreement with the foreign policy of the United States."

Secretary of Defense George Marshall supported Truman's decision to replace MacArthur. Marshall believed MacArthur's public statements to the press were intolerable.

MacArthur receives a hero's welcome in New York City upon his return from the Far East.

A large segment of the American public did not support Truman's decision to fire MacArthur. The White House received piles of critical telegrams and letters. In the first week after MacArthur's dismissal, seventy-eight thousand pieces of mail were sent to the president, twenty to one against his action. A Gallup poll showed that 69 percent of the American people backed MacArthur, while a mere 28 percent supported Harry Truman.

After being fired, MacArthur returned to the United States for the first time in many years. He received a tumultuous reception in San Francisco and a huge ticker-tape parade in New York City.

The Old Soldier Does Not Fade Away

MacArthur's many friends and political allies in government invited the general to address a joint session of Congress. In the course of his speech, MacArthur made his famous, stirring statement: "Old soldiers never die, they just fade away. And like the old soldier of that ballad, I now close my military career and just fade away—an old soldier who tried to do his duty as God gave him the light to see that duty. Good-bye."

But MacArthur had no intention of fading away. He wanted to challenge Truman for the presidency. Republican supporters were so upset about MacArthur's dismissal that they held two months of congressional hearings regarding MacArthur's handling of the Korean conflict. By questioning MacArthur, Republicans intended to justify the actions of their hero and to cast doubt upon the leadership of Truman and of his Democratic administration.

Under close scrutiny in closed Senate hearings, however, MacArthur's luster began to dim. During his testimony, he revealed that he had often disobeyed the orders of the president.

He continued to deny any responsibility for the terrible loss of American lives in November and December 1951. Most important, it became clear that MacArthur's policies could lead the United States to the brink of World War III.

MacArthur's testimony diminished the anger many people felt toward President Truman. The public gained respect for Truman's upholding of the principle of presidential control of the military. Truman's appointment of Matthew Ridgway as commander of the UN forces became more acceptable to MacArthur's friends, especially since Ridgway provided the successes the president and the American public craved.

CHAPTER SIX

A Conflict of Limited Motion

The military situation that Ridgway faced in 1951 was not favorable. UN forces had suffered a long retreat, and the morale of the troops was very low.

Ridgway arrived in Korea with a reputation for being a flamboyant and aggressive leader. He was determined to use that reputation to help turn the defeated UN forces into a worthy army.

A bit of dramatics on the part of the general set the stage for the campaigns of 1951. He first appeared before his troops wearing a hand grenade attached to one shoulder strap of his parachute harness and a first-aid kit to the other. As one writer reported, "The first-aid kit was often mistaken for another hand grenade. The widespread belief that Ridgway wore grenades on both chest harnesses led the GIs to nickname him Old Iron Tits."

Ridgway did not perform such antics simply for the sake of publicity. He wanted to convince his troops that they now had a field commander who was determined to fight and who would be victorious. He had a big task before him. The general described the disarray he first saw in Korea:

> I drove out north of Seoul and into a dismaying spectacle. ROK soldiers by truckloads were streaming south, without order, without arms, without leaders, in full retreat. Some came on foot or in commandeered vehicles of every sort. They had just one aim—to get as far away from the Chinese as possible. They had thrown their rifles and pistols away and had abandoned all artillery, mortars, machine guns, every crew-served weapon.

The Eighth Army needed inspiration and leadership. Ridgway provided both. He had to replace the defeatist attitude of the disorganized military units with optimism. Ridgway's behavior and determination to be victorious instilled a new aggressive spirit and a sense of pride into the UN forces.

Ridgway established specific assembly points, called straggler posts, beyond the Han River, south of the line of retreat. These were military encampments where disorganized units were provided with warm food, new equipment, and discipline by U.S. military police. He also instituted a system of "R and R" (rest and recreation)—a five day trip to Japan—on a rotating basis for soldiers and officers alike. The anticipation of this break greatly bolstered the spirits of the UN forces and increased their willingness to fight. Under Ridgway's strict and confident leadership, the troops were transformed into a tough fighting army. They never again retreated in disarray in Korea.

With Ridgway in command, the army, the Joint Chiefs of Staff, the president, and the State Department were all in agreement regarding the UN goals in Korea. The UN army, which had been driven far south of Seoul, would make its way back to the 38th parallel. There, it would establish a strong position. It would grind down the enemy by waging a defensive war until the enemy decided to negotiate an end to the conflict. The UN army was not going to attempt to reunite Korea. The troops were there to reestablish the 38th parallel as the dividing line between North Korea and South Korea.

Ridgway proceeded to do just that. He studied the tactics employed by the Chinese. He knew that the poorly armed soldiers of the Chinese armies were most successful at night. In the dark, they caught UN forces off guard, infiltrated the UN lines, and attacked small units from all directions. The general also recognized that the Chinese could not sustain their attacks indefinitely. They had to fall back, regroup, and replace their dead and wounded with fresh troops. Ridgway reorganized his units and used strategies to counter these Chinese tactics. In particular, Ridgway denied the enemy time to reorganize and regroup after an attack.

Taking the Offensive

Then, UN forces—including ROK, American, Dutch, French, British, Thai, Turkish, and other national units—took the offensive instead of waiting to be attacked. In late January 1951, the UN army slowly began to move north in a campaign called Operation Thunderbolt. Ridgway's strategy was to inflict huge losses on the enemy through combined land and air attacks. His objective was to reduce Chinese morale and to drive the communists beyond the 38th parallel.

Matthew B. Ridgway

Lt. Gen. Matthew B. Ridgway (1895–1965) took over General MacArthur's duties in Japan and Korea after President Truman fired MacArthur in April 1951. Ridgway was a natural selection for the post since he had an outstanding reputation and the full confidence of Secretary of Defense George Marshall.

A West Point graduate, Ridgway had had the opportunity to work under Marshall on four separate occasions. Marshall had been extremely impressed with Ridgway's skill and professionalism and "had come to regard him somewhat like an adopted son."

Ridgway became famous for his daring exploits during World War II. Long fascinated with German airborne operations, Ridgway was appointed the commander of the 82d Infantry Division and turned that, the 101st, and several others into enormously effective airborne divisions. Despite his age and previous injuries, Ridgway himself made five parachute jumps, including one into Normandy on D day.

Ridgway commanded his troops from the front lines. Frequently wounded, he refused hospitalization, preferring to remain with his troops, who performed magnificently in battle.

Massive firepower from planes (left) and howitzers (right) allowed UN forces to slow the communist advance.

In 1950, the soldiers had advanced in long columns that were easy targets for enemy sharpshooters hiding in the hills. In 1951, UN forces advanced on a broad front in units. Chinese ambushes, so successful during the earlier retreats, no longer worked as effectively. Ridgway took care that his forces fortified their advance positions strongly to prevent the enemy from breaking through the lines. Ridgway reported that this advance was "far different from the reckless and uncoordinated plunge toward the Yalu," which had ended in disaster for the UN armies.

The Chinese met the advancing forces on February 11, throwing most of their troops against the South Korean divisions near the town of Hoengsong. Although many ROK units were forced back, some UN forces, particularly some French and British units, formed tightly closed circles near Chipyong-ni. They held onto the town, an important juncture of roads, despite repeated attacks during the next several days by overwhelming enemy forces. The British and French troops caused five thousand Chinese casualties in three days.

The repulse of the Chinese attack in February 1951 was aided by numerous war planes. The planes supported the land troops by bombing Chinese troops and raking them with fire. They also dropped napalm on the Chinese. Massive firepower from heavy artillery that were rushed to the front, combined with air and land attacks, enabled the UN forces to use technology to make up for what they lacked in troop strength.

After stopping the Chinese February offensive, UN forces resumed their northward march. During the next six weeks, Ridgway succeeded in recovering most of South Korea for the United Nations.

The steadily advancing UN forces threatened to control most of the roads in the region and to prevent the escape of Chinese troops stationed in Seoul. Realizing this, the Chinese decided to evacuate the South Korean capital.

Securing South Korea's Capital

UN troops entered Seoul once again on March 14, 1951. The civilian population of the capital had suffered terribly during the Chinese occupation and retreat. Rutherford Poasts of the United Press traveled with the Eighth Army and poignantly described one of the conflict's tragedies: "Telephone and power lines festooned the streets or hung from shattered poles which resembled grotesque Christmas trees. A tiny figure stumbled down the street. Her face, arms and legs were burned and almost eaten away by the fragments of an American white phosphorous shell. She was blind, but somehow alive." Mercifully, having changed hands four times in the past nine months, the South Korean capital and its population never again fell to enemy forces.

By early June 1951, UN forces reached the 38th parallel, where they dug in. Over the next few months, UN troops advanced north of the 38th parallel in order to strengthen strategic portions of the UN front line. These were followed by short, sharp enemy counterattacks. But the 38th parallel, lying across the steep and complex mountain chain of central Korea, essentially became the dividing line between the opposing armies.

UN forces used heavy artillery (left) to destroy enemy positions along the 38th parallel. This allowed easier access to UN paratroopers (right).

Napalm

UN forces fighting in Korea confronted enemy armies far larger than their own. To increase their chances of success, particularly after the entrance of the Chinese communists, the UN troops used very powerful modern weapons. They hoped these weapons would be effective against the huge enemy armies. One of these was a chemical substance called napalm.

Napalm is a thick mixture of jellied gasoline. Ironically, much of the napalm used during the Korean War was produced in Japan and was used against towns and factories that had been built by the Japanese when they controlled Korea.

Napalm was dropped from planes that were able to carry two 150-pound napalm bombs. The bombs could be dropped from as low as two hundred feet. The effect of the napalm on military machinery was devastating. The substance was capable of destroying anything within an area 275 feet long and 100 feet wide of the drop site. The chemical was especially effective against armored tanks because it was able to eat through metal, but it was also used against trains, trucks, troops, airfields, railroads, tunnels, and harbor facilities.

Unfortunately, napalm was also used against villages when UN forces suspected that enemy troops were being sheltered by the inhabitants. The effects of napalm on the human body are horrible almost beyond description. The fire resulting from the napalm bomb explosions burns off the flesh.

On December 1, 1950, UN planes accidently dropped napalm on retreating UN troops. One soldier remembered that the napalm exploded in the middle of a group of soldiers. "I don't know how in the world the flames missed me. In my lifetime, I'll never know. Men all around me were burned. They lay rolling in the snow. Men I knew, marched and fought with begged me to shoot them....I couldn't....It was terrible. Where the napalm had burned the skin to a crisp, it would be peeled back from the face, arms, legs...like fried potato chips."

Napalm was used both in the Vietnam and Korean wars with terrible effects. Here, a small child with napalm burns.

Residents of Seoul search through rubble (left). Much of the city was leveled after repeated bombing raids.

After June 1951, there were no more dramatic advances and retreats along the length of the peninsula. The UN army never again faced the threat of being driven out of Korea by superior forces. Likewise, the North Korean capital of Pyongyang and the Yalu River were no longer considered to be the primary UN objectives. The war became a conflict of limited motion.

Like the UN forces to the south, the Chinese and North Korean forces to the north of the 38th parallel also "dug in." Since UN bombing had destroyed almost all the towns of North Korea, the Chinese and North Koreans dug intricate systems of tunnels for protection. These were covered with logs and mud, which made their detection from the air difficult. And frontal assaults were deadly to the attacker.

All along the width of Korea in that second summer of the conflict, the soldiers of the two enemy forces prepared to "hang on" for as long as their political leaders thought necessary. The situation resembled the trench warfare of World War I, in which two massed armies faced each other across trenches and took up the grim task of slaughtering one another in limited but costly engagements.

The Punchbowl

The Korean War became a war of short thrusts to obtain limited objectives. One of the most famous and most bloody Korean engagements occurred as General Ridgway attempted to straighten and strengthen a sag in the UN defensive line between

August and October 1951. In an area known as the Punchbowl, extremely high hills enabled the enemy to look down on UN fortifications and military preparations. Ridgway wanted the enemy removed both from the Punchbowl and the high hills surrounding the deep depression.

The Chinese and North Koreans were dug in deeply. UN war planes fired on the hills and dropped napalm but did little damage either to the deep bunkers or to the mine fields the enemy had placed all over the area.

These positions would have to be taken through deadly frontal assaults. UN forces made repeated charges against the bunkers, only to be driven back by grenades and automatic weapons. The slaughter became so great that the reporters covering the action called the hills near the Punchbowl Heartbreak Hill and Bloody Ridge.

On October 13, 1951, the French battalion had the honor of storming the last stronghold on Heartbreak Hill. The ridge commanding the high ground surrounding the Punchbowl was finally in UN hands.

But the losses had been staggering. In the action taking Heartbreak Hill alone, the UN troops suffered more than thirty-seven hundred casualties. The Chinese and North Koreans sustained estimated losses as high as twenty-five thousand. In all, during the summer of 1951, UN forces sustained sixty thousand casualties, twenty-two thousand of which were Americans. It is estimated that the Chinese and North Koreans suffered seventy thousand casualties.

UN forces watch the entrance to a tunnel near Heartbreak Hill (left). UN troops make their way toward Seoul (right).

Numerous UN bombing raids destroyed much of North Korea.

What took place along the ridge near the Punchbowl was repeated hundreds of times on different hills over the next two years. UN war planes flew thousands of missions and dropped many thousands of tons of bombs and napalm in support of the ground troops. The air attacks destroyed fields, farm animals, and people. They destroyed villages suspected of permitting the enemy to hide in their huts during the day. The repeated bombings turned the landscape of most of North Korea into a nightmare of destruction. One soldier described the scene as a "brown landscape with skeletons of trees clawing the air."

The actual cost in lives in this phase of the conflict was far higher than during the previous period of vast sweeps of armies. The soldiers on both sides died from the cold as well as from battle wounds as they tried to gain control of the North Korean hills. Then, many hills would be abandoned by the army commanders as soon as the last enemy soldiers surrendered or were killed.

The human suffering, particularly in the third winter of the war, was enormous. Sgt. Glenn Hubenette of F Company in the Seventh Infantry Division sent a letter to his mother describing the soldiers' physical and psychological pain:

Tanner and I watched while the doctors removed big, jagged pieces of metal and fatigue jacket cloth from the hole in Lieutenant Miller's side. What a bloody mess. Next, we were sent to a hospital set up in a schoolhouse that was handling a lot of men. One young lad sitting next to me in the hallway was hysterical. He'd shot himself through the foot. When I'd been treated, a doctor major began work on the young GI. Told the kid if he had his way, he'd let him bleed to death, and that the guy didn't belong in the same army with men who'd been legitimately wounded. The major might as well have saved his breath; the GI didn't hear a word he'd said. Who knew what the kid had gone through before he shot his foot?

Medics in this evacuation hospital prepare a patient for surgery (right). One soldier comforts another over the death of a friend (below).

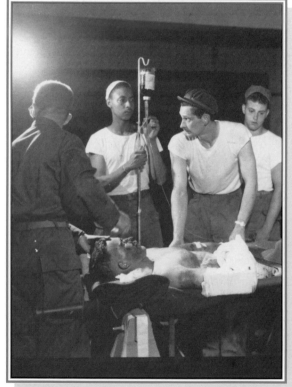

Later I learned his company had lost twenty-six men on the slopes of that big horseshoe-shaped ridge.

The horrors of the war were carved into the memories of its survivors. Sgt. Ed Hendrick of F Company in the Fifth Cavalry provides an unforgettable image of the results of winter fighting in Korea:

> Worse thing I ever saw in my life—twenty, thirty trucks lined up carrying American dead of Chipyong-ni. Columns of deuce-and-a-halfs, one behind the other. The corpses couldn't be flattened out, because they were frozen the way the men were when they'd been killed. Blankets couldn't cover the arms and legs sticking in every direction. Bodies on top of bodies, fitted together like a jigsaw puzzle. The whole valley around Chipyong-ni was full of dead people.

These scenes of death and destruction slowly wore down the morale of the UN soldiers, who knew that these military actions were intended to be used only as bargaining chips in the political negotiations taking place elsewhere.

American soldiers help a wounded comrade (left). A South Korean girl carries a baby past an M-26 tank (right).

CHAPTER SEVEN

Peace Negotiations

Peace talks usually take place after an enemy has been defeated and the killing has ceased. Toward the end of the Korean conflict, however, neither of these conditions existed. The war was fought only as a campaign within the larger context of the ongoing Cold War between the Soviet Union and the United States. The communists wanted to see if the West would respond to the challenge in Korea. Truman and the United Nations were determined not to let the challenge go unanswered.

The two sides had fought to a stalemate along the former border between North Korea and South Korea, the 38th parallel. By the summer of 1951, it was clear that unless each side wanted to escalate the scale of the conflict, the Cold War would not be decided in Korea. So both sides faced the difficult task of restoring peace.

The UN leadership and the Soviet Union agreed that the time had come to talk about peace terms. As the major supplier of financial, military, and political assistance to communist China and to North Korea, the Soviets played a major role in bringing the communists to the conference table.

During May and June 1951, secret and unofficial discussions took place between representatives of the United States and the Soviet Union. These behind-the-scenes contacts resulted in an announcement on June 23, 1951, by the Soviet Union that it was in favor of opening peace discussions between North Koreans, communist China, and a representative of the United Nations.

Those talks began on July 10, 1951, at a small town called Kaesong, just north of the 38th parallel and within reach of enemy lines. On several occasions, UN negotiators on their way to the talks were harassed by North Korean soldiers. As a result, the conference site was moved to a safer spot, a town called Panmunjom, just west of Kaesong but outside the reach of communist forces.

The UN negotiating team was headed by Adm. Turner Joy, General Ridgway's naval chief. He and his staff confronted two Chinese generals, Hsieh Fang and Teng Hua, and three North Korean generals, Nam Il, Lee Sang Cho, and Chang Pyong San.

The Most Bizarre Events in History

The peace talks were among the most prolonged and bizarre events in diplomatic history. The talks were carried out while the most vicious and destructive phases of the conflict occurred. From July until November 1951, during the battles on the ridge lines, there were nearly 60,000 UN casualties, of which more than 22,000 were American, and almost 234,000 North Korean and Chinese casualties. The talks dragged on for nearly twenty-five months. Admiral Joy described them as proceeding "with all the speed of a stiff concrete mix."

The talks were stalled by disagreements over the shape of the negotiating table, by the intrusion of armed soldiers, and by the occasional walkout of angry negotiators. But peace was so difficult to achieve because of the substantial differences that continued to divide the two warring sides. Like everything else about the Korean War, the peace talks were simply another manifestation of the Cold War. Neither side wished to give the enemy an advantage in this ongoing ideological conflict.

All the items on the agenda created major disputes. One issue was the location of the final line dividing North and South Korea. UN troops had moved north of the 38th parallel along a line of ridges in order to hold strong positions on high ground. Admiral Joy wanted to keep that advanced line as the new boundary. The communists found this line unacceptable. So the two armies continued to battle for the land between the ridges and the 38th parallel for another two years. The communists also opposed the idea of a twenty-mile-wide demilitarized zone between the two countries that the UN negotiators wanted as a buffer area against future attack.

The UN negotiating team anticipated the continued presence of a UN peacekeeping force in Korea after the fighting ceased. The communists adamantly opposed the ongoing presence of "foreign troops" on Korean soil.

Jacob Malik

In the summer of 1951, the American government wished to begin peace discussions with the North Koreans. American State Department officials believed that they could make contact with the Chinese communists and North Koreans through a Soviet representative. Jacob Malik was a possible choice since he was the Soviet ambassador to the United Nations at the time. After some discussions between an unofficial American representative and Malik at Malik's summer house on Long Island, New York, the Soviet government agreed to permit peace discussions to begin. This agreement was signaled by an announcement Malik made on United Nations radio on June 23, 1951. Malik gave his support for "discussions between the belligerents for a cease-fire and an armistice providing for mutual withdrawal from the 38th parallel."

Since the Cold War relations between the United States and the Soviet Union were so hostile, the United States had to verify that the announcement was authentic. Staff at the American embassy in Moscow asked Soviet foreign minister Andrey Gromyko if the broadcast had the support of the Soviet government. Gromyko confirmed that the statement reflected the official Soviet position regarding peace talks.

A North Korean soldier has surrendered to UN forces (left). Communist forces returned these UN POWs (right) to the UN front lines.

Prisoners of War

Finally, the peace talks bogged down over the emotionally charged issue of what to do with prisoners of war. The United Nations wanted all prisoners to be free to choose where they wanted to live. The communists feared freedom of choice would result in the refusal of communist prisoners to return to their countries.

For a brief moment in 1952, Americans believed that the dreary conflict would end. Dwight D. Eisenhower was elected to succeed Harry Truman as president. One of Eisenhower's campaign promises had been to break through the deadlocked negotiations at Panmunjom. So in November 1952, Eisenhower fulfilled his campaign promise to "go to Korea." But his three-day visit did nothing to speed up the peace talks. Instead, Eisenhower discovered, as Truman already knew, that the peace talks were tightly bound up in the ideological rhetoric of the Cold War. It would require an extraordinary event to break the deadlock.

As a result, the talks dragged on endlessly while thousands of men on both sides died, not only on the battlefields of Korea but also in the prison camps. In fact, the fate of the prisoners of war (POWs) often seemed more important in the negotiations than that of the soldiers on the front lines.

Admiral Joy was especially concerned about freeing UN POWs because reports of their treatment were horrifying. United Nations representatives knew they had to get these POWs out soon or they would not survive.

Communist Atrocities

There were thousands of POW lives at stake. During the first months of the Korean crisis, both sides captured many prisoners as the armies moved swiftly across the Korean peninsula. When the UN troops moved north in September and October 1950, they began to discover how prisoners were treated by the enemy. Advance units came upon the bodies of dead prisoners. The hands of these UN prisoners had been tied behind their backs, and most of the men had been shot in the back of the head.

The worst single atrocity of the war came to light as the Eighth Army moved north from Pyongyang, the North Korean capital, in October 1950. Brig. Gen. Frank A. Allen, Jr., and his party discovered a sad and sickening sight near a railroad tunnel near Myongucham, about five miles northwest of the town of Sunchon.

U.S. Marines guard North Korean prisoners (above). Captured communist guerrillas (right) eat at a UN camp.

The UN POW camp at Pusan contained North Korean and communist Chinese prisoners (left). A captured North Korean soldier holds a picture of Soviet leader Joseph Stalin (right).

General Allen came upon the bodies of sixty-five American POWs who had been murdered, starved to death, or died of disease as the North Koreans hurried north with their prisoners, trying to escape the bombs of the planes that accompanied the advancing UN army.

General Allen also discovered twenty-three more Americans near starvation who had escaped from the North Koreans and who told the general the ghastly details of their experience. One survivor related the following account:

> Two trains, each carrying about one hundred and fifty American POWs left Pyongyang on October 17, 1950, crawling slowly and repairing the heavily broken tracks as they went. These were the survivors of a group of three hundred and seventy Americans the North Koreans had marched north from Seoul shortly after the Inchon landing. Each day five or six Americans died of dysentery, starvation, or exposure. Their bodies were removed from the train. A few Americans escaped along the way. On October 20th, while a paratroop drop was in progress, the second of the two trains remained in the Myongucham tunnel. It still had about one hundred Americans, crowded into open coal gondolas and boxcars. That evening, the North Korean guards took the

Americans in three groups to get their evening meal. The North Koreans shot them down as they waited for it. Most of the Americans who survived did so by feigning death. The guards and the train left that night.

These atrocities were not isolated events. Much later, the world would learn about the horrible conditions in which UN POWs lived and died in the Chinese prison camps near the Yalu River. PFC Lawrence Bailey of C Company in the Thirty-second Infantry was one of the few POWs to survive to tell the story of those camps. He describes in graphic detail the conditions under which he lived in "Death Valley," a POW camp consisting of a group of unheated huts run by the Chinese communists:

> After a month or so in Death Valley, people who had frozen body parts actually started pulling them off—toes and fingertips and ears—and putting them in a pot the Koreans left in our huts. I don't know what the Koreans did with those rotting parts of human beings. I do know that some of our people were talking about eating them. I hope no one ever did, but I wouldn't be surprised if one had. You get a little crazy when you are starving. I lost all the toes on my

An anticommunist POW (left), just released from a North Korean POW camp. A woman weeps at the sight of dead political prisoners, killed by the North Koreans (right).

Brainwashing

Brainwashing developed out of the treatment of UN POWs by the communist Chinese during the Korean War. During brainwashing, POWs were subjected to systematic indoctrination intended to undermine allegiance to their country.

Once under Chinese control, the POWs were generally not in danger of being murdered. But many prisoners were subjected to brainwashing techniques that consisted of various kinds of mental torture. The prisoners were required to hear endless repetitions of communist slogans and anti-Western propaganda. The Chinese also tried to stir up racial tensions among the prisoners. They hoped that this would break up the loyalties within national groups.

Many POWs were offered extra rations and promised less harsh living conditions if they accepted the communist propaganda. The communists worked hard in attempting to brainwash their prisoners. Each POW who converted was viewed by the communists as a great propaganda victory. The converts were forced to write and speak out against the West or sign "peace petitions" urging the stopping of the war. In this way, the communists were able to publicize the conversion of their POWs.

After the Korean War, many mental health workers studied the effectiveness of these brainwashing techniques. Most studies suggest that perhaps 12 percent of all POWs "actively and consistently" resisted all efforts at mind control. The great majority "cooperated in indoctrination and interrogation sessions in a passive sort of way, although there was a tendency to refuse to say anything obviously traitorous." When all POWs were finally exchanged, it was learned that only twenty-one Americans and one British serviceman had refused to go home to the West.

In a similar way, the POWs under UN control were encouraged to reject communism. But there is no evidence that they were subjected to the systematic and relentless brainwashing that accompanied imprisonment of the UN troops by the communist Chinese.

right foot and four from my left and I lost the little finger of my right hand.

By the time we had been in Death Valley for a month people were dying, two and three every night, mostly from starvation and untreated wounds. But there were deaths from other causes, too. The lice were thick, and we had cases of what must have been typhus. It was hard to be sure. There were no medics with us. In a way, the dead helped the rest of us stay alive. We would keep the bodies covered up for as long as we could so that we could collect the dead men's rations.

The knowledge of the dismal fate of the many captives still unaccounted for made their liberation a major priority at the peace talks.

South Korean Atrocities

Unfortunately, the North Koreans and Chinese communists were not the only ones who mistreated their POWs. The South Koreans displayed the same brutality toward their North Korean captives. They starved and beat North Korean prisoners, and many were hanged instead of being transported to POW camps in the south.

There were also many reports of American mistreatment of POWs, although not of deliberate slaughter. A British officer reported after the conflict that "some GIs treated their prisoners like animals, showing little respect even for the wounded." The Americans captured tens of thousands of communist soldiers. Often, the troops were ill prepared to deal with the many logistical problems of providing food, housing, clothing, and adequate supervision for the captives. The UN troops frequently resorted to harsh behavior in order to keep the prisoners marching south.

When the peace talks began, some hope existed that the POW problem would be resolved quickly. Expectations for the early release of the UN POWs soon vanished, however. They had become pawns in the Cold War.

The Chinese used all kinds of brutal measures to "brainwash" their UN captives into refusing to return to the West. They hoped that if large numbers of UN POWs refused to go home, the communists would achieve a great propaganda victory. In fact, some POWs pretended to show interest in communism in order to lighten the terms of their imprisonment.

At the same time, the communists knew that tens of thousands of their own POWs did not want to return to China and to North Korea. The communist brainwashing campaign was designed to counter any propaganda advantage the West would gain from communist defections. But to ensure that the number of defections would be small, the communists insisted on the immediate return of all prisoners of war.

Joseph Stalin

Joseph Stalin (1879–1953) was the Soviet premier at the time of the outbreak of the Korean War. He had been a close colleague of Vladimir Ilyich Lenin, the founder of the Soviet communist state. After Lenin died in 1924, Stalin gradually built up his own political power. When he felt his position was relatively secure, he brutally destroyed all internal opposition to his regime throughout the 1930s.

After World War II, Stalin's armies seized central and eastern Europe to establish a security zone to protect the Soviet Union against further aggression.

The United States and its allies believed that Stalin was the moving force behind the increasingly aggressive Soviet threat to the West. It was widely believed during the 1950s that the Soviet Union, not communist China, had first given permission to the North Koreans to invade South Korea. It was also believed that Stalin was happy to supply arms to the Chinese and North Koreans in order to continue the drain of UN strength, which would leave Stalin free to pursue aggression in western Europe.

Western observers of the Soviet Union began to notice that Stalin appeared to be making plans to begin a new purge of potential opponents within the Soviet Union. As a result, Soviet interest in continuing the Korean conflict declined. When Stalin died on March 5, 1953, his successors were concerned with consolidating their own positions and relaxing tensions with the West. With Stalin gone, less assistance could be expected from Soviet allies, and the possibility of bringing the Korean War to a conclusion increased.

Joseph Stalin often resorted to brutal methods to control political opponents during World War II.

This demand placed President Truman and the United Nations negotiating team in a terrible dilemma. Truman wanted all UN soldiers returned immediately, but he also wanted to allow Chinese and North Korean POWs to defect if they so wished.

Truman believed that part of the purpose of the peace talks should be to prevent communist prisoners from being returned against their will. The president therefore announced that the United States would not compel anticommunist North Koreans and Chinese POWs to return to their homes. Truman wrote: "Just as I had always insisted that we could not abandon the South Koreans who had stood by us and freedom, so I now refused to agree to any solution that provided for the return against their will of prisoners of war to communist domination. We will not buy an armistice by turning over human beings for slaughter or slavery."

As the negotiators at Panmunjom argued over the fate of the POWs, the huge prisoner cages on Koje Island became military and propaganda battlefields. Prisoner cages were large compounds surrounded by wire fences. Although each compound was designed to hold forty-five hundred prisoners, some held as many as nine thousand POWs. The entire prisoner compound was run by the UN forces. There, the Chinese and North Korean prisoners who wanted to return home fought against those who wanted to remain in South Korea or go to the island of Formosa.

To gain control of this situation, communist propaganda agents let themselves be captured and sent to Koje Island, where they worked to organize the communist prisoner cages.

The Cages at Koje

In the spring of 1953, tensions rose both in the cages and between the prisoners and their guards. The violence in the cages increased. Finally, a major crisis erupted. Thousands of communist prisoners rioted, and inmates armed with homemade weapons attacked American soldiers trying to control the situation.

Brig. Gen. Francis T. Dodd, commander of the POW camp, went into the cages to talk to the prisoners. He was seized as a hostage and then tried as a criminal by the communist POWs. Dodd was forced to confess that he had committed terrible crimes, such as the use of machine guns, poison gas, and torture on Koje. He even admitted that Americans had used germ warfare against the communist soldiers. Although none of this was true, the Chinese publicized the event to humiliate the Americans.

General Ridgway then took control. He sent in Gen. Mark Clark to stop the riots. Clark called in the battle-seasoned soldiers of the Eighty-second Airborne Division to replace the guards on Koje Island. They gained the release of General Dodd, restored order in the prison compounds, broke up the cages into smaller compounds, and took steps to keep outside agitators from China from getting to the ringleaders of the riots.

Suddenly, much of the furor died down both on Koje and at Panmunjom. The death in the Soviet Union of Joseph Stalin on March 5, 1953, drastically affected the Soviet Union's attitude toward the peace talks. Stalin's successors were eager to impress the West with their willingness to deal more openly with the United States and its allies.

Operation Little Switch

In April 1953, the United Nations and communist negotiators were able to come to the first agreement over POWs, called Operation Little Switch. Under the agreement, sick and wounded POWs would be exchanged. Many of the other outstanding POW issues were resolved within the next three months.

This soldier was one of the first released during Operation Little Switch.

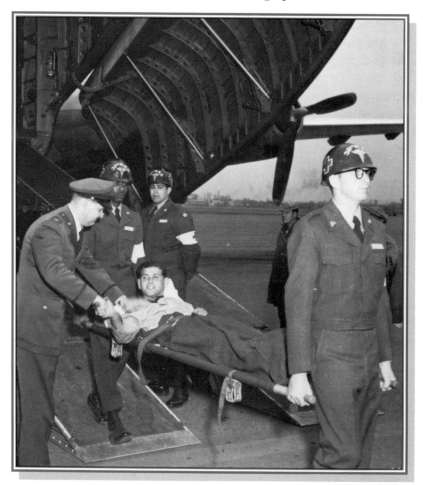

By June, both sides had agreed to establish a Neutral Nations Repatriation Commission to oversee the return of POWs. Those prisoners who wished to return to their home were free to do so within sixty days. Those who refused repatriation, or a return to their country, were turned over to the commission, consisting of Indian troops. The troops would protect the POWs for ninety days, during which time communist educators were available in case the POWs wished to change their mind.

Many feared that the exchanges would not be carried out smoothly. Operation Big Switch, the major exchange of POWs, began in August 1953. UN prisoners were turned over to the UN command, and those North Koreans and communist Chinese who wished were permitted to stay in South Korea or go to Formosa.

At last, the Korean War was over. An armistice was signed on July 27, 1953. Korea remained divided at the 38th parallel, roughly where the conflict started three long years before. North Korea ended up being about twenty-one thousand square miles smaller than it had been in June 1950. The political differences between the two halves of Korea continued to poison relations between them.

Negotiators at the Panmunjom conference (left). This soldier was released during Operation Big Switch (right).

Results of the Korean War

On July 27, 1953, the guns of war finally fell silent over Korea. The financial cost of the conflict had been staggering. The United States alone spent more than sixty-seven billion dollars to keep South Korea independent. The human cost was almost beyond measure. More than 1 million Koreans were dead, and 2 million were homeless. Continuous bombings had left North Korea a wasteland. Chinese losses were also enormous, with well over 1 million dead, but the exact number of total Chinese casualties would never be known. The United States, too, suffered tragic human losses, with more than 140,000 casualties, including 33,000 known dead. Nearly two-thirds of the UN forces held in Chinese and North Korean prison camps never returned. Of the few who did, most suffered the lingering effects of malnutrition, mistreatment, and physical disfigurement from the loss of body parts.

When the United States came to the aid of South Korea in 1950, Americans had no idea the conflict would be so costly. The United States simply accepted the responsibility of fighting in defense of the independence of South Korea. President Truman decided, and the American people supported his decision, to drive the North Korean armies out of South Korea. When UN units recrossed the 38th parallel in September 1950, they achieved this objective.

If the conflict had ended there, it could have been a victory. Instead, the war dragged on for almost two more bloody years

Korean civilians, killed near Yongsan. More than one million Koreans died during the Korean War.

when the United Nations decided to reunite all of Korea under a democratic government by force. The UN dreadfully underestimated the Chinese.

From this perspective, the conflict was a failure both for the military and political leaders of the United States. They did not calculate the costs involved. They failed to understand that communist China would not tolerate the presence of UN forces on its border. They did not recognize that China would sustain any losses necessary to prevent that from happening and that the Soviet Union would support China with enormous amounts of supplies and diplomatic assistance.

The anticommunist hysteria in the United States during and after the war, however, led American leaders and the public to believe they needed to oppose communism everywhere. To do this, the United States stockpiled conventional weapons and nuclear weapons. Many leaders came to the conclusion that atomic warfare was a cheap and effective alternative to the costly losses sustained in the Korean conflict.

Unfortunately, the Soviet Union, too, responded by stockpiling nuclear weapons. And so began the race to build bigger and more efficient atomic weapons, resulting in the "balance of terror" phase of the Cold War that began after the Korean conflict.

The world seemed more dangerous and confusing to Americans after the Korean War than it had in 1950. Many were angered because they did not understand the new rules of warfare in the atomic age. Americans were asked to pay heavy taxes to provide for both conventional weapons and to keep up the nuclear race with the Soviets. Americans could not easily accept the notion of the need to fight a war for ideological reasons, such as fighting a communist regime in another country.

For all these reasons, the American public turned its back on the conflict in Korea long before it was over. There were no protests to "bring the boys home." The boys were simply forgotten. Along with the veterans, the lessons of the conflict were also forgotten. In fact, at almost the same moment that the last Korean veterans returned home as unsung heroes, other American advisers were committing the country to a similar conflict in another distant Asian country called Vietnam.

Glossary

C-47   extremely versatile airplane used by UN forces to carry in supplies and to airlift out wounded soldiers during the Korean War.

Inchon landing   landing made behind North Korean lines by the UN armies on September 15, 1950.

Kaesong   first site of the peace talks.

Koje Island   small island off the southern coast of South Korea where communist prisoners of war were kept by UN forces.

Operation Big Switch   the name given to the exchange of prisoners of war that took place in August 1953.

Operation Little Switch   the name given to the exchange of sick and wounded prisoners of war in the spring of 1953.

Panmunjom   the site of most of the peace talks that finally brought the Korean War to an end.

Punchbowl   a depression in a highly mountainous area just north of the 38th parallel that was the scene of very bloody fighting in 1951.

Pyongyang   the capital city of North Korea.

Seoul   the capital city of South Korea; the capital of all of Korea before World War II.

Thirty-eighth Parallel   the dividing line established by the United States and the Soviet Union to separate North Korea and South Korea at the conclusion of World War II.

Yalu River   the border between the Chinese province of Manchuria and North Korea that the Chinese were committed to protect from UN forces.

Works Consulted

Dean Acheson, *Present at the Creation, My Years in the State Department*. New York: Norton and Company, 1969.

Bein Alexander, *Korea, The First War We Lost*. New York: Hippocrene Books, 1986.

Harry J. Carman, Harold C. Syrett, and Bernard W. Wishy, *A History of the American People*. Vol. 2. New York: Knopf, 1967.

Blair Clay, *The Forgotten War: America in Korea 1950-53*. New York: Times Books, 1987.

James Cotton and Ian Neary, eds. *The Korean War in History*. Atlantic Highlands, N.J.: Humanities Press International, Inc., 1989.

Rosemary Foot, *A Substitute for Victory*. Ithaca: Cornell University Press, 1990.

Louis J. Halle, *The Cold War as History*. New York: Harper & Row, 1967.

Richard P. Hallion, *The Naval Air War in Korea*. Baltimore: The Nautical and Aviation Publishing Company of America, 1986.

Donald Knox, *The Korean War: Uncertain Victory*. San Diego: Harcourt, Brace, Jovanovich, 1988.

Ralph B. Levering, *The Cold War, 1945–1987*. Arlington Heights, IL: Harlan Davidson, 1988.

Callum A. MacDonald, *Korea, The War Before Vietnam*. New York: The Free Press, 1986.

Michael Schaller, *Douglas MacArthur: The Far Eastern General*. New York: Oxford University Press, 1989.

Robert Smith, *MacArthur in Korea: The Naked Emperor*. New York: Simon & Schuster, 1982.

John Spanier, *American Foreign Policy Since World War II*. Washington, DC: Congressional Quarterly, Inc., 1988.

Bernard A. Weisberger, *Cold War Cold Peace*. New York: American Heritage Press, 1985.

Howard Zinn, *Postwar America*. New York: Bobb-Merrill Company, Inc., 1982.

Index

Photo Credits

Cover photo: AP/Wide World

AP/Wide World Photos, 18

Harry S Truman Library, 33

Library of Congress, 63, 84

Paule Loring. By permission of the *Providence Evening Bulletin,* 62

National Archives, 9, 15, 17 (all), 22 (both), 23, 26, 27 (both), 28 (both), 29 (both), 31 (left), 35, 36 (all), 40 (all), 41, 43, 44, 47 (all), 48 (both), 57, 59, 66, 68 (both), 69 (both), 71 (both), 72 (left), 73 (all), 74 (both), 75 (both), 78 (both), 79 (both), 80 (both), 81 (both), 86, 87 (both), 89

Reuters/Bettmann, 30

UPI/Bettmann Newsphotos, 21, 31 (right), 32, 52, 53, 54, 64, 70, 72 (right)

Vicky. By permission of the *London Evening Standard,* 58

About the Author

Deborah Bachrach was born and raised in New York City, where she received her undergraduate education. She earned a Ph.D. in history from the University of Minnesota. Dr. Bachrach has taught at the University of Minnesota, at St. Francis College in Joliet, Illinois, and at Queens College in New York City. In addition, she has worked for many years in the fields of medical research and public-policy development. Dr. Bachrach has written two books for the *America's Wars* series.